# *POEMS.*

BY

W. D. HOWELLS.

BOSTON:
JAMES R. OSGOOD AND COMPANY,
Late Ticknor & Fields, and Fields, Osgood, & Co.
1873.

Entered according to Act of Congress, in the year 1873,
BY JAMES R. OSGOOD AND COMPANY,
in the Office of the Librarian of Congress, at Washington.

University Press: Welch, Bigelow, & Co.,
Cambridge.

# CONTENTS.

# THE PILOT'S STORY.

I.

IT was a story the pilot told, with his back to his hearers, —
Keeping his hand on the wheel and his eye on the globe of the jack-staff,
Holding the boat to the shore and out of the sweep of the current,
Lightly turning aside for the heavy logs of the drift-wood,
Widely shunning the snags that made us sardonic obeisance.

II.

All the soft, damp air was full of delicate perfume
From the young willows in bloom on either bank of the river, —
Faint, delicious fragrance, trancing the indolent senses
In a luxurious dream of the river and land of the lotus.

Not yet out of the west the roses of sunset were
withered;
In the deep blue above light clouds of gold and
of crimson
Folated in slumber serene; and the restless river
beneath them
Rushed away to the sea with a vision of rest in
its bosom;
Far on the eastern shore lay dimly the swamps of
the cypress;
Dimly before us the islands grew from the river's
expanses, —
Beautiful, wood-grown isles, with the gleam of the
swart inundation
Seen through the swaying boughs and slender
trunks of their willows;
And on the shore beside us the cotton-trees rose
in the evening,
Phantom-like, yearningly, wearily, with the in-
scrutable sadness
Of the mute races of trees. While hoarsely the
steam from her 'scape-pipes
Shouted, then whispered a moment, then shouted
again to the silence,
Trembling through all her frame with the mighty
pulse of her engines,
Slowly the boat ascended the swollen and broad
Mississippi,

Bank-full, sweeping on, with tangled masses of drift-wood,
Daintily breathed about with whiffs of silvery vapor,
Where in his arrowy flight the twittering swallow alighted,
And the belated blackbird paused on the way to its nestlings.

III.

It was the pilot's story: — "They both came aboard there, at Cairo,
From a New Orleans boat, and took passage with us for Saint Louis.
She was a beautiful woman, with just enough blood from her mother
Darkening her eyes and her hair to make her race known to a trader:
You would have thought she was white. The man that was with her, — you see such, —
Weakly good-natured and kind, and weakly good-natured and vicious,
Slender of body and soul, fit neither for loving nor hating.
I was a youngster then, and only learning the river, —
Not over-fond of the wheel. I used to watch them at monte,

Down in the cabin at night, and learned to know
all of the gamblers.
So when I saw this weak one staking his money
against them,
Betting upon the turn of the cards, I knew what
was coming:
*They* never left their pigeons a single feather to
fly with.
Next day I saw them together, — the stranger and
one of the gamblers:
Picturesque rascal he was, with long black hair
and moustaches,
Black slouch hat drawn down to his eyes from his
villanous forehead.
On together they moved, still earnestly talking in
whispers,
On toward the forecastle, where sat the woman
alone by the gangway.
Roused by the fall of feet, she turned, and, be-
holding her master,
Greeted him with a smile that was more like a
wife's than another's,
Rose to meet him fondly, and then, with the
dread apprehension
Always haunting the slave, fell her eye on the
face of the gambler, —
Dark and lustful and fierce and full of merciless
cunning.

Something was spoken so low that I could not
hear what the words were;
Only the woman started, and looked from one to
the other,
With imploring eyes, bewildered hands, and a
tremor
All through her frame: I saw her from where I
was standing, she shook so.
'Say! is it so?' she cried. On the weak, white
lips of her master
Died a sickly smile, and he said, 'Louise, I have
sold you.'
God is my judge! May I never see such a look
of despairing,
Desolate anguish, as that which the woman cast
on her master,
Griping her breast with her little hands, as if he
had stabbed her,
Standing in silence a space, as fixed as the Indian
woman
Carved out of wood, on the pilot-house of the old
Pocahontas!
Then, with a gurgling moan, like the sound in the
throat of the dying,
Came back her voice, that, rising, fluttered,
through wild incoherence,
Into a terrible shriek that stopped my heart while
she answered: —

'Sold me ? sold me ? sold — And you promised
to give me my freedom ! —
Promised me, for the sake of our little boy in
Saint Louis !
What will you say to our boy, when he cries for
me there in Saint Louis ?
What will you say to our God ? — Ah, you have
been joking ! I see it ! —
No ? God ! God ! He shall hear it, — and all of
the angels in heaven, —
Even the devils in hell ! — and none will believe
when they hear it !
Sold me ! ' — Her voice died away with a wail,
and in silence
Down she sank on the deck, and covered her face
with her fingers."

IV.

In his story a moment the pilot paused, while we
listened
To the salute of a boat, that, rounding the point
of an island,
Flamed toward us with fires that seemed to burn
from the waters, —
Stately and vast and swift, and borne on the heart
of the current.
Then, with the mighty voice of a giant challenged
to battle,

Rose the responsive whistle, and all the echoes of island,
Swamp-land, glade, and brake replied with a myriad clamor,
Like wild birds that are suddenly startled from slumber at midnight,
Then were at peace once more; and we heard the harsh cries of the peacocks
Perched on a tree by a cabin-door, where the white-headed settler's
White-headed children stood to look at the boat as it passed them,
Passed them so near that we heard their happy talk and their laughter.
Softly the sunset had faded, and now on the eastern horizon
Hung, like a tear in the sky, the beautiful star of the evening.

V.

Still with his back to us standing, the pilot went on with his story: —
"All of us flocked round the woman. The children cried, and their mothers
Hugged them tight to their breasts; but the gambler said to the captain, —
'Put me off there at the town that lies round the bend of the river.

Here, you! rise at once, and be ready now to go
with me.'
Roughly he seized the woman's arm and strove to
uplift her.
She — she seemed not to heed him, but rose like
one that is dreaming,
Slid from his grasp, and fleetly mounted the steps
of the gangway,
Up to the hurricane-deck, in silence, without lam-
entation.
Straight to the stern of the boat, where the wheel
was, she ran, and the people
Followed her fast till she turned and stood at bay
for a moment,
Looking them in the face, and in the face of the
gambler.
Not one to save her, — not one of all the compas-
sionate people!
Not one to save her, of all the pitying angels in
heaven!
Not one bolt of God to strike him dead there
before her!
Wildly she waved him back, we waiting in silence
and horror.
Over the swarthy face of the gambler a pallor of
passion
Passed, like a gleam of lightning over the west in
the night-time.

White, she stood, and mute, till he put forth his
hand to secure her;
Then she turned and leaped, — in mid-air fluttered a moment, —
Down then, whirling, fell, like a broken-winged
bird from a tree-top,
Down on the cruel wheel, that caught her, and
hurled her, and crushed her,
And in the foaming water plunged her, and hid
her forever."

VI.

Still with his back to us all the pilot stood, but
we heard him
Swallowing hard, as he pulled the bell-rope for
stopping. Then, turning, —
"This is the place where it happened," brokenly
whispered the pilot.
"Somehow, I never like to go by here alone in
the night-time."
Darkly the Mississippi flowed by the town that lay
in the starlight,
Cheerful with lamps. Below we could hear them
reversing the engines,
And the great boat glided up to the shore like a
giant exhausted.
Heavily sighed her pipes. Broad over the swamps
to the eastward

Shone the full moon, and turned our far-trembling wake into silver.
All was serene and calm, but the odorous breath of the willows
Smote with a mystical sense of infinite sorrow upon us.

## FORLORN.

I.

RED roses, in the slender vases burning,
  Breathed all upon the air, —
The passion and the tenderness and yearning,
  The waiting and the doubting and despair.

II.

Still with the music of her voice was haunted,
  Through all its charméd rhymes,
The open book of such a one as chanted
  The things he dreamed in old, old summer-times.

III.

The silvern chords of the piano trembled
  Still with the music wrung
From them ; the silence of the room dissembled
  The closes of the songs that she had sung.

IV.

The languor of the crimson shawl's abasement, —
  Lying without a stir

Upon the floor, — the absence at the casement,
The solitude and hush were full of her.

V.

Without, and going from the room, and never
Departing, did depart
Her steps; and one that came too late forever
Felt them go heavy o'er his broken heart.

VI.

And, sitting in the house's desolation,
He could not bear the gloom,
The vanishing encounter and evasion
Of things that were and were not in the room.

VII.

Through midnight streets he followed fleeting visions
Of faces and of forms;
He heard old tendernesses and derisions
Amid the sobs and cries of midnight storms.

VIII.

By midnight lamps, and from the darkness under
That lamps made at their feet,
He saw sweet eyes peer out in innocent wonder,
And sadly follow after him down the street.

IX.

The noonday crowds their restlessness obtruded
  Between him and his quest;
At unseen corners jostled and eluded,
  Against his hand her silken robes were pressed.

X.

Doors closed upon her; out of garret casements
  He knew she looked at him;
In splendid mansions and in squalid basements,
  Upon the walls he saw her shadow swim.

XI.

From rapid carriages she gleamed upon him,
  Whirling away from sight;
From all the hopelessness of search she won him
  Back to the dull and lonesome house at night.

XII.

Full early into dark the twilights saddened
  Within its closéd doors;
The echoes, with the clock's monotony maddened,
  Leaped loud in welcome from the hollow floors;

XIII.

But gusts that blew all day with solemn laughter
  From wide-mouthed chimney-places,

And the strange noises between roof and rafter,
The wainscot clamor, and the scampering races

XIV.

Of mice that chased each other through the chambers,
And up and down the stair,
And rioted among the ashen embers,
And left their frolic footprints everywhere, —

XV.

Were hushed to hear his heavy tread ascending
The broad steps, one by one,
And toward the solitary chamber tending,
Where the dim phantom of his hope alone

XVI.

Rose up to meet him, with his growing nearer,
Eager for his embrace,
And moved, and melted into the white mirror,
And stared at him with his own haggard face.

XVII.

But, turning, he was 'ware *her* looks beheld him
Out of the mirror white ;
And at the window yearning arms she held him,
Out of the vague and sombre fold of night.

XVIII.

Sometimes she stood behind him, looking over
His shoulder as he read;
Sometimes he felt her shadowy presence hover
Above his dreamful sleep, beside his bed;

XIX.

And rising from his sleep, her shadowy presence
Followed his light descent
Of the long stair; her shadowy evanescence
Through all the whispering rooms before him went.

XX.

Upon the earthy draught of cellars blowing
His shivering lamp-flame blue,
Amid the damp and chill, he felt her flowing
Around him from the doors he entered through.

XXI.

The spiders wove their webs upon the ceiling;
The bat clung to the wall;
The dry leaves through the open transom stealing,
Skated and danced adown the empty hall.

XXII.

About him closed the utter desolation,
About him closed the gloom;

B

The vanishing encounter and evasion
  Of things that were and were not in the room

XXIII.

Vexed him forever; and his life forever
  Immured and desolate,
Beating itself, with desperate endeavor,
  But bruised itself, against the round of fate.

XXIV.

The roses, in their slender vases burning,
  Were quenchéd long before;
A dust was on the rhymes of love and yearning;
  The shawl was like a shroud upon the floor.

XXV.

Her music from the thrilling chords had perished;
  The stillness was not moved
With memories of cadences long cherished,
  The closes of the songs that she had loved.

XXVI.

But not the less he felt her presence never
  Out of the room depart;
Over the threshold, not the less, forever
  He felt her going on his broken heart.

## PLEASURE-PAIN.

"Das Vergnügen ist Nichts als ein höchst angenehmer Schmerz."—HEINRICH HEINE.

I.

FULL of beautiful blossoms
  Stood the tree in early May:
Came a chilly gale from the sunset,
  And blew the blossoms away;

Scattered them through the garden,
  Tossed them into the mere:
The sad tree moaned and shuddered,
  "Alas! the Fall is here."

But all through the glowing summer
  The blossomless tree throve fair,
And the fruit waxed ripe and mellow,
  With sunny rain and air;

And when the dim October
  With golden death was crowned,
Under its heavy branches
  The tree stooped to the ground.

In youth there comes a west-wind
  Blowing our bloom away, —
A chilly breath of Autumn
  Out of the lips of May.

We bear the ripe fruit after, —
  Ah, me! for the thought of pain! —
We know the sweetness and beauty
  And the heart-bloom never again.

II.

One sails away to sea,
  One stands on the shore and cries;
The ship goes down the world, and the light
  On the sullen water dies.

The whispering shell is mute,
  And after is evil cheer:
She shall stand on the shore and cry in vain,
  Many and many a year.

But the stately, wide-winged ship
  Lies wrecked on the unknown deep;
Far under, dead in his coral bed,
  The lover lies asleep.

III.

Through the silent streets of the city,
In the night's unbusy noon,
Up and down in the pallor
Of the languid summer moon,

I wander, and think of the village,
And the house in the maple-gloom,
And the porch with the honeysuckles
And the sweet-brier all abloom.

My soul is sick with the fragrance
Of the dewy sweet-brier's breath :
O darling! the house is empty,
And lonesomer than death!

If I call, no one will answer;
If I knock, no one will come :
The feet are at rest forever,
And the lips are cold and dumb.

The summer moon is shining
So wan and large and still,
And the weary dead are sleeping
In the graveyard under the hill.

IV.

We looked at the wide, white circle
 Around the Autumn moon,
And talked of the change of weather :
 It would rain, to-morrow, or soon.

And the rain came on the morrow,
 And beat the dying leaves
From the shuddering boughs of the maples
 Into the flooded eaves.

The clouds wept out their sorrow ;
 But in my heart the tears
Are bitter for want of weeping,
 In all these Autumn years.

V.

The bobolink sings in the meadow,
 The wren in the cherry-tree :
Come hither, thou little maiden,
 And sit upon my knee ;

And I will tell thee a story
 I read in a book of rhyme ;
I will but fain that it happened
 To me, one summer-time,

When we walked through the meadow,
  And she and I were young.
The story is old and weary
  With being said and sung.

The story is old and weary:
  Ah, child! it is known to thee.
Who was it that last night kissed thee
  Under the cherry-tree?

VI.

Like a bird of evil presage,
  To the lonely house on the shore
Came the wind with a tale of shipwreck,
  And shrieked at the bolted door,

And flapped its wings in the gables,
  And shouted the well-known names,
And buffeted the windows
  Afeard in their shuddering frames.

It was night, and it is morning,—
  The summer sun is bland,
The white-cap waves come rocking, rocking,
  In to the summer land.

The white-cap waves come rocking, rocking,
  In the sun so soft and bright,

And toss and play with the dead man
  Drowned in the storm last night.

VII.

I remember the burning brushwood,
  Glimmering all day long
Yellow and weak in the sunlight,
  Now leaped up red and strong,

And fired the old dead chestnut,
  That all our years had stood,
Gaunt and gray and ghostly,
  Apart from the sombre wood ;

And, flushed with sudden summer,
  The leafless boughs on high
Blossomed in dreadful beauty
  Against the darkened sky.

We children sat telling stories,
  And boasting what we should be,
When we were men like our fathers,
  And watched the blazing tree,

That showered its fiery blossoms,
  Like a rain of stars, we said,
Of crimson and azure and purple.
  That night, when I lay in bed,

I could not sleep for seeing,
  Whenever I closed my eyes,
The tree in its dazzling splendor
  Against the darkened skies.

I cannot sleep for seeing,
  With closéd eyes to-night,
The tree in its dazzling splendor
  Dropping its blossoms bright;

And old, old dreams of childhood
  Come thronging my weary brain,
Dear, foolish beliefs and longings:
  I doubt, are they real again?

It is nothing, and nothing, and nothing,
  That I either think or see:
The phantoms of dead illusions
  To-night are haunting me.

## IN AUGUST.

ALL the long August afternoon,
The little drowsy stream
Whispers a melancholy tune,
As if it dreamed of June
And whispered in its dream.

The thistles show beyond the brook
Dust on their down and bloom,
And out of many a weed-grown nook
The aster-flowérs look
With eyes of tender gloom.

The silent orchard aisles are sweet
With smell of ripening fruit.
Through the sere grass, in shy retreat,
Flutter, at coming feet,
The robins strange and mute.

There is no wind to stir the leaves,
The harsh leaves overhead;
Only the querulous cricket grieves,
And shrilling locust weaves
A song of Summer dead.

## THE EMPTY HOUSE.

THE wet trees hang above the walks
  Purple with damps and earthish stains,
  And strewn by moody, absent rains
With rose-leaves from the wild-grown stalks.

Unmown, in heavy, tangled swaths,
  The ripe June-grass is wanton blown;
  Snails slime the untrodden threshold-stone;
Along the sills hang drowsy moths.

Down the blank visage of the wall,
  Where many a wavering trace appears,
  Like a forgotten trace of tears,
From swollen eaves the slow drops crawl.

Where everything was wide before,
  The curious wind, that comes and goes,
  Finds all the latticed windows close,
Secret and close the bolted door.

And with the shrewd and curious wind,
  That in the archéd doorway cries,

  And at the bolted portal tries,
And harks and listens at the blind, —

Forever lurks my thought about,
  And in the ghostly middle-night
  Finds all the hidden windows bright,
And sees the guests go in and out,

And lingers till the pallid dawn,
  And feels the mystery deeper there
  In silent, gust-swept chambers, bare,
With all the midnight revel gone ;

But wanders through the lonesome rooms,
  Where harsh the astonished cricket calls,
  And, from the hollows of the walls
Vanishing, start unshapen glooms ;

And lingers yet, and cannot come
  Out of the drear and desolate place,
  So full of ruin's solemn grace,
And haunted with the ghost of home.

## BUBBLES.

I.

I STOOD on the brink in childhood,
And watched the bubbles go
From the rock-fretted, sunny ripple
To the smoother tide below ;

And over the white creek-bottom,
Under them every one,
Went golden stars in the water,
All luminous with the sun.

But the bubbles broke on the surface,
And under, the stars of gold
Broke ; and the hurrying water
Flowed onward, swift and cold.

II.

I stood on the brink in manhood,
And it came to my weary brain,
And my heart, so dull and heavy
After the years of pain, —

That every hollowest bubble
  Which over my life had passed
Still into its deeper current
  Some heavenly gleam had cast;

That, however I mocked it gayly,
  And guessed at its hollowness,
Still shone, with each bursting bubble,
  One star in my soul the less.

## LOST BELIEFS.

ONE after one they left us;
The sweet birds out of our breasts
Went flying away in the morning:
Will they come again to their nests?

Will they come again at nightfall,
With God's breath in their song?
Noon is fierce with the heats of summer,
And summer days are long!

O my Life, with thy upward liftings,
Thy downward-striking roots,
Ripening out of thy tender blossoms
But hard and bitter fruits!—

In thy boughs there is no shelter
For the birds to seek again.
The desolate nest is broken
And torn with storms and rain!

## LOUIS LEBEAU'S CONVERSION.

YESTERDAY, while I moved with the languid crowd on the Riva,
Musing with idle eyes on the wide lagoons and the islands,
And on the dim-seen seaward glimmering sails in the distance,
Where the azure haze, like a vision of Indian-Summer,
Haunted the dreamy sky of the soft Venctian December, —
While I moved unwilled in the mellow warmth of the weather,
Breathing air that was full of Old World sadness and beauty
Into my thought came this story of free, wild life in Ohio,
When the land was new, and yet by the Beautiful River
Dwelt the pioneers and Indian hunters and boatmen.

Pealed from the campanili, responding from island to island,
Bells of that ancient faith whose incense and solemn devotions
Rise from a hundred shrines in the broken heart of the city;
But in my revery heard I only the passionate voices
Of the people that sang in the virgin heart of the forest.
Autumn was in the land, and the trees were golden and crimson,
And from the luminous boughs of the over-elms and the maples
Tender and beautiful fell the light in the worshippers' faces,
Softer than lights that stream through the saints on the windows of churches,
While the balsamy breath of the hemlocks and pines by the river
Stole on the winds through the woodland aisles like the breath of a censer.
Loud the people sang old camp-meeting anthems that quaver
Quaintly yet from lips forgetful of lips that have kissed them;

Loud they sang the songs of the Sacrifice and Atonement,
And of the end of the world, and the infinite terrors of Judgment : —
Songs of ineffable sorrow, and wailing, compassionate warning
Unto the generations that hardened their hearts to their Savior ;
Songs of exultant rapture for them that confessed him and followed,
Bearing his burden and yoke, enduring and entering with him
Into the rest of his saints, and the endless reward of the blessed.
Loud the people sang ; but through the sound of their singing
Broke inarticulate cries and moans and sobs from the mourners,
As the glory of God, that smote the apostle of Tarsus,
Smote them and strewed them to earth like leaves in the breath of the whirlwind.

Hushed at last was the sound of the lamentation and singing ;
But from the distant hill the throbbing drum of the pheasant

Shook with its heavy pulses the depths of the listening silence,
When from his place arose a white-haired exhorter, and faltered:
"Brethren and sisters in Jesus! the Lord hath heard our petitions,
So that the hearts of his servants are awed and melted within them, —
Even the hearts of the wicked are touched by his infinite mercy.
All my days in this vale of tears the Lord hath been with me,
He hath been good to me, he hath granted me trials and patience;
But this hour hath crowned my knowledge of him and his goodness.
Truly, but that it is well this day for me to be with you,
Now might I say to the Lord, — 'I know thee, my God, in all fulness;
Now let thy servant depart in peace to the rest thou hast promised!'"

Faltered and ceased. And now the wild and jubilant music
Of the singing burst from the solemn profound of the silence,

Surged in triumph, and fell, and ebbed again into silence.

Then from the group of the preachers arose the greatest among them, —
He whose days were given in youth to the praise of the Savior,
He whose lips seemed touched, like the prophet's of old, from the altar,
So that his words were flame, and burned to the hearts of his hearers,
Quickening the dead among them, reviving the cold and the doubting.
There he charged them pray, and rest not from prayer while a sinner
In the sound of their voices denied the Friend of the sinner:
" Pray till the night shall fall, — till the stars are faint in the morning, —
Yea, till the sun himself be faint in that glory and brightness,
Faint in the light which shall dawn in mercy for penitent sinners."
Kneeling, he led them in prayer; and the quick and sobbing responses
Spake how their souls were moved with the might and the grace of the Spirit.

Then while the converts recounted how God had
chastened and saved them, —
Children, whose golden locks yet shone with the
lingering effulgence
Of the touches of Him who blessed little children
forever;
Old men, whose yearning eyes were dimmed with
the far-streaming brightness
Seen through the opening gates in the heart of
the heavenly city, —
Stealthily through the harking woods the lengthen-
ing shadows
Chased the wild things to their nests, and the
twilight died into darkness.

Now the four great pyres that were placed
there to light the encampment,
High on platforms raised above the people, were
kindled.
Flaming aloof, as it were the pillar by night in the
Desert
Fell their crimson light on the lifted orbs of the
preachers,
Fell on the withered brows of the old men, and
Israel's mothers,
Fell on the bloom of youth, and the earnest devo-
tion of manhood,

Fell on the anguish and hope in the tearful eyes of the mourners.
Flaming aloof, it stirred the sleep of the luminous maples
With warm summer-dreams, and faint, luxurious languor.
Near the four great pyres the people closed in a circle,
In their midst the mourners, and, praying with them, the exhorters,
And on the skirts of the circle the unrepentant and scorners, —
Ever fewer and sadder, and drawn to the place of the mourners,
One after one, by the prayers and tears of the brethren and sisters,
And by the Spirit of God, that was mightily striving within them,
Till at the last alone stood Louis Lebeau, unconverted.

Louis Lebeau, the boatman, the trapper, the hunter, the fighter,
From the unlucky French of Gallipolis he descended,
Heir to Old World want and New World love of adventure.

Vague was the life he led, and vague and grotesque were the rumors
Through which he loomed on the people, — the hero of mythical hearsay,
Quick of hand and of heart, impatient, generous, Western,
Taking the thought of the young in secret love and in envy.
Not less the elders shook their heads and held him for outcast,
Reprobate, roving, ungodly, infidel, worse than a Papist,
With his whispered fame of lawless exploits at St. Louis,
Wild affrays and loves with the half-breeds out on the Osage,
Brawls at New Orleans, and all the towns on the rivers,
All the godless towns of the many-ruffianed rivers.
Only she who loved him the best of all, in her loving
Knew him the best of all, and other than that of the rumors.
Daily she prayed for him, with conscious and tender effusion,
That the Lord would convert him. But when her father forbade him

Unto her thought, she denied him, and likewise
held him for outcast,
Turned her eyes when they met, and would not
speak, though her heart broke.

Bitter and brief his logic that reasoned from
wrong unto error:
"This is their praying and singing," he said,
"that makes you reject me, —
You that were kind to me once. But I think my
fathers' religion,
With a light heart in the breast and a friendly
priest to absolve one,
Better than all these conversions that only be-
wilder and vex me,
And that have made men so hard and women
fickle and cruel.
Well, then, pray for my soul, since you would not
have spoken to save me, —
Yes; for I go from these saints to my brethren
and sisters, the sinners."
Spoke and went, while her faint lips fashioned
unuttered entreaties, —
Went, and came again in a year at the time of
the meeting,
Haggard and wan of face, and wasted with passion
and sorrow.

Dead in his eyes was the careless smile of old, and its phantom
Haunted his lips in a sneer of restless, incredulous mocking.
Day by day he came to the outer skirts of the circle,
Dwelling on her, where she knelt by the white-haired exhorter, her father,
With his hollow looks, and never moved from his silence.

Now, where he stood alone, the last of impenitent sinners,
Weeping, old friends and comrades came to him out of the circle,
And with their tears besought him to hear what the Lord had done for them.
Ever he shook them off, not roughly, nor smiled at their transports.
Then the preachers spoke and painted the terrors of Judgment,
And of the bottomless pit, and the flames of hell everlasting.
Still and dark he stood, and neither listened nor heeded;
But when the fervent voice of the white-haired exhorter was lifted,

Fell his brows in a scowl of fierce and scornful
rejection.
"Lord, let this soul be saved!" cried the fervent
voice of the old man;
"For that the Shepherd rejoiceth more truly for
one that hath wandered,
And hath been found again, than for all the
others that strayed not."

Out of the midst of the people, a woman old
and decrepit,
Tremulous through the light, and tremulous into
the shadow,
Wavered toward him with slow, uncertain paces
of palsy,
Laid her quivering hand on his arm and brokenly
prayed him:
"Louis Lebeau, I closed in death the eyes of your
mother.
On my breast she died, in prayer for her fatherless
children,
That they might know the Lord, and follow him
always, and serve him.
O, I conjure you, my son, by the name of your
mother in glory,
Scorn not the grace of the Lord!" As when a
summer-noon's tempest

Breaks in one swift gush of rain, then ceases and
gathers
Darker and gloomier yet on the lowering front of
the heavens,
So broke his mood in tears, as he soothed her, and
stilled her entreaties,
And so he turned again with his clouded looks to
the people.

Vibrated then from the hush the accents of
mournfullest pity, —
His who was gifted in speech, and the glow of the
fires illumined
All his pallid aspect with sudden and marvellous
splendor :
"Louis Lebeau," he spake, "I have known you
and loved you from childhood ;
Still, when the others blamed you, I took your
part, for I knew you.
Louis Lebeau, my brother, I thought to meet you
in heaven,
Hand in hand with her who is gone to heaven
before us,
Brothers through her dear love! I trusted to
greet you and lead you
Up from the brink of the River unto the gates of
the City.

Lo! my years shall be few on the earth. O my brother,
If I should die before you had known the mercy of Jesus,
Yea, I think it would sadden the hope of glory within me!"

Neither yet had the will of the sinner yielded an answer;
But from his lips there broke a cry of unspeakable anguish,
Wild and fierce and shrill, as if some demon within him
Rent his soul with the ultimate pangs of fiendish possession;
And with the outstretched arms of bewildered imploring toward them,
Death-white unto the people he turned his face from the darkness.

Out of the sedge by the creek a flight of clamorous killdees
Rose from their timorous sleep with piercing and iterant challenge,
Wheeled in the starlight, and fled away into distance and silence.
White in the vale lay the tents, and beyond them glided the river,

Where the broadhorn * drifted slow at the will of
the current,
And where the boatman listened, and knew not
how, as he listened,
Something touched through the years the old lost
hopes of his childhood, —
Only his sense was filled with low, monotonous
murmurs,
As of a faint-heard prayer, that was chorused with
deeper responses.

Not with the rest was lifted her voice in the
fervent responses,
But in her soul she prayed to Him that heareth
in secret,
Asking for light and for strength to learn his will
and to do it:
"O, make me clear to know if the hope that rises
within me
Be not part of a love unmeet for me here, and
forbidden!
So, if it be not that, make me strong for the evil
entreaty
Of the days that shall bring me question of self
and reproaches,

* The old-fashioned flatboats were so called.

When the unrighteous shall mock, and my brethren and sisters shall doubt me!
Make me worthy to know thy will, my Savior, and do it!"
In her pain she prayed, and at last, through her mute adoration,
Rapt from all mortal presence, and in her rapture uplifted,
Glorified she rose, and stood in the midst of the people,
Looking on all with the still, unseeing eyes of devotion, —
Vague, and tender, and sweet, as the eyes of the dead, when we dream them
Living and looking on us, but they cannot speak, and we cannot, —
Knowing only the peril that threatened his soul's unrepentance,
Knowing only the fear and error and wrong that withheld him,
Thinking, "In doubt of me, his soul had perished forever!"
Touched with no feeble shame, but trusting her power to save him,
Through the circle she passed, and straight to the side of her lover,
Took his hand in her own, and mutely implored him an instant,

Answering, giving, forgiving, confessing, beseeching him all things;
Drew him then with her, and passed once more through the circle
Unto her place, and knelt with him there by the side of her father,
Trembling as women tremble who greatly venture and triumph, —
But in her innocent breast was the saint's sublime exultation.

So was Louis converted; and though the lips of the scorners
Spared not in after years the subtle taunt and derision
(What time, meeker grown, his heart held his hand from its answer),
Not the less lofty and pure her love and her faith that had saved him,
Not the less now discerned was her inspiration from heaven
By the people, that rose, and embracing and weeping together,
Poured forth their jubilant songs of victory and of thanksgiving,
Till from the embers leaped the dying flame to behold them,

And the hills of the river were filled with reverberant echoes, —
Echoes that out of the years and the distance stole to me hither,
While I moved unwilled in the mellow warmth of the weather ;
Echoes that mingled and fainted and fell with the fluttering murmurs
In the hearts of the hushing bells, as from island to island
Swooned the sound on the wide lagoons into palpitant silence.

## CAPRICE.

I.

SHE hung the cage at the window:
  "If he goes by," she said,
"He will hear my robin singing,
  And when he lifts his head,
I shall be sitting here to sew,
And he will bow to me, I know."

The robin sang a love-sweet song,
  The young man raised his head;
The maiden turned away and blushed:
  "I am a fool!" she said,
And went on broidering in silk
A pink-eyed rabbit, white as milk.

II.

The young man loitered slowly
  By the house three times that day;
She took her bird from the window:
  "He need not look this way."
She sat at her piano long,
And sighed, and played a death-sad song.

But when the day was done, she said,
  "I wish that he would come!
Remember, Mary, if he calls
  To-night — I 'm not at home."
So when he rang, she went — the elf! —
She went and let him in herself.

III.

They sang full long together
  Their songs love-sweet, death-sad;
The robin woke from his slumber,
  And rang out, clear and glad.
"Now go!" she coldly said; "'t is late;"
And followed him — to latch the gate.

He took the rosebud from her hair,
  While, "You shall not!" she said;
He closed her hand within his own,
  And, while her tongue forbade,
Her will was darkened in the eclipse
Of blinding love upon his lips.

## SWEET CLOVER.

—— My letters back to me."

I.

I KNOW they won the faint perfume,
  That to their faded pages clings,
  From gloves, and handkerchiefs, and things
Kept in the soft and scented gloom

Of some mysterious box — poor leaves
  Of summer, now as sere and dead
  As any leaves of summer shed
From crimson boughs when autumn grieves!

The ghost of fragrance! Yet I thrill
  All through with such delicious pain
  Of soul and sense, to breathe again
The sweet that haunted memory still.

And under these December skies,
  As bland as May's in other climes,
  I move, and muse my idle rhymes
And subtly sentimentalize.

I hear the music that was played, —
  The songs that silence knows by heart ! —
  I see sweet burlesque feigning art,
The careless grace that curved and swayed

Through dances and through breezy walks ;
  I feel once more the eyes that smiled,
  And that dear presence that beguiled
The pauses of the foolish talks,

When this poor phantom of perfume
  Was the Sweet Clover's living soul,
  And breathed from her as if it stole,
Ah, heaven ! from her heart in bloom !

II.

We have not many ways with pain :
  We weep weak tears, or else we laugh ;
  I doubt, not less the cup we quaff,
And tears and scorn alike are vain.

But let me live my quiet life ;
  I will not vex my calm with grief,
  I only know the pang was brief,
And there an end of hope and strife.

And thou? I put the letters by:
  In years the sweetness shall not pass;
  More than the perfect blossom was
I count its lingering memory.

Alas! with Time dear Love is dead,
  And not with Fate. And who can guess
  How weary of our happiness
We might have been if we were wed?

Venice, 1861.

## THE ROYAL PORTRAITS.

(AT LUDWIGSHOF.)

I.

CONFRONTING each other the pictures stare
  Into each other's sleepless eyes;
  And the daylight into the darkness dies,
From year to year in the palace there:
  But they watch and guard that no device
Take either one of them unaware.

Their majesties the king and the queen,
  The parents of the reigning prince:
  Both put off royalty many years since,
With life and the gifts that have always been
  Given to kings from God, to evince
His sense of the mighty over the mean.

I cannot say that I like the face
  Of the king; it is something fat and red;
  And the neck that lifts the royal head
Is thick and coarse; and a scanty grace
  Dwells in the dull blue eyes that are laid
Sullenly on the queen in her place.

He must have been a king in his day
  'T were well to pleasure in work and sport :
  One of the heaven-anointed sort
Who ruled his people with iron sway,
  And knew that, through good and evil report,
God meant him to rule and them to obey.

There are many other likenesses
  Of the king in his royal palace there ;
  You find him depicted everywhere, —
In his robes of state, in his hunting-dress,
  In his flowing wig, in his powdered hair, —
A king in all of them, none the less ;

But most himself in this on the wall
  Over against his consort, whose
  Laces, and hoops, and high-heeled shoes
Make her the finest lady of all
  The queens or courtly dames you choose,
In the ancestral portrait hall.

A glorious blonde : a luxury
  Of luring blue and wanton gold,
  Of blanchéd rose and crimson bold,
Of lines that flow voluptuously
  In tender, languorous curves to fold
Her form in perfect symmetry.

She might have been false. Of her withered dust
  There scarcely would be enough to write
  Her guilt in now ; and the dead have a right
To our lenient doubt if not to our trust :
  So if the truth cannot make her white,
Let us be as merciful as we — must.

II.

The queen died first, the queen died young,
  But the king was very old when he died,
  Rotten with license, and lust, and pride ;
And the usual Virtues came and hung
  Their cypress wreaths on his tomb, and wide
Throughout his kingdom his praise was sung.

How the queen died is not certainly known,
  And faithful subjects are all forbid
  To speak of the murder which some one did
One night while she slept in the dark alone :
  History keeps the story hid,
And Fear only tells it in undertone.

Up from your startled feet aloof,
  In the famous Echo-Room, with a bound
  Leaps the echo, and round and round
Beating itself against the roof, —
  A horrible, gasping, shuddering sound, —
Dies ere its terror can utter proof

Of that it knows. A door is fast,
  And none is suffered to enter there.
  His sacred majesty could not bear
To look at it toward the last,
  As he grew very old. It opened where
The queen died young so many years past.

III.

How the queen died is not certainly known ;
  But in the palace's solitude
  A harking dread and horror brood,
And a silence, as if a mortal groan
  Had been hushed the moment before, and would
Break forth again when you were gone.

The present king has never dwelt
  In the desolate palace. From year to year
  In the wide and stately garden drear
The snows and the snowy blossoms melt
  Unheeded, and a ghastly fear
Through all the shivering leaves is felt.

By night the gathering shadows creep
  Along the dusk and hollow halls,
  And the slumber-broken palace calls
With stifled moans from its nightmare sleep ;
  And then the ghostly moonlight falls
Athwart the darkness brown and deep.

At early dawn the light wind sighs,
  And through the desert garden blows
  The wasted sweetness of the rose;
At noon the feverish sunshine lies
  Sick in the walks. But at evening's close,
When the last, long rays to the windows rise,

And with many a blood-red, wrathful streak
  Pierce through the twilight glooms that blur
  His cruel vigilance and her
Regard, they light fierce looks that wreak
  A hopeless hate that cannot stir,
A voiceless hate that cannot speak

In the awful calm of the sleepless eyes;
  And as if she saw her murderer glare
  On her face, and he the white despair
Of his victim kindle in wild surmise,
  Confronted the conscious pictures stare, —
And their secret back into darkness dies.

## THE FAITHFUL OF THE GONZAGA.*

I.

FEDERIGO, the son of the Marquis,
  Downcast, through the garden goes:
He is hurt with the grace of the lily,
  And the beauty of the rose.

For what is the grace of the lily
  But her own slender grace?
And what is the rose's beauty
  But the beauty of her face? —

Who sits beside her window
  Waiting to welcome him,

* The author of this ballad has added a thread of evident love-story to a most romantic incident of the history of Mantua, which occurred in the fifteenth century. He relates the incident so nearly as he found it in the *Cronache Montovane*, that he is ashamed to say how little his invention has been employed in it. The hero of the story, Federigo, became the third Marquis of Mantua, and was a prince greatly beloved and honored by his subjects.

That comes so lothly toward her
  With his visage sick and dim.

"Ah! lily, I come to break thee!
  Ah! rose, a bitter rain
Of tears shall beat thy light out
  That thou never burn again!"

II.

Federigo, the son of the Marquis,
  Takes the lady by the hand:
"Thou must bid me God-speed on a journey,
  For I leave my native land.

"From Mantua to-morrow
  I go, a banished man;
Make me glad for truth and love's sake
  Of my father's curse and ban.

"Our quarrel has left my mother
  Like death upon the floor;
And I come from a furious presence
  I never shall enter more.

"I would not wed the woman
  He had chosen for my bride,
For my heart had been before him,
  With his statecraft and his pride.

"I swore to him by my princehood
  In my love I would be free;
And I swear to thee by my manhood,
  I love no one but thee.

"Let the Duke of Bavaria marry
  His daughter to whom he will:
There where my love was given
  My word shall be faithful still.

"There are six true hearts will follow
  My truth wherever I go,
And thou equal truth wilt keep me
  In welfare and in woe."

The maiden answered him nothing
  Of herself, but his words again
Came back through her lips like an echo
  From an abyss of pain;

And vacantly repeating
  "In welfare and in woe,"
Like a dream from the heart of fever
  From her arms she felt him go.

III.

Out of Mantua's gate at daybreak
  Seven comrades wander forth

On a path that leads at their humor,
East, west, or south, or north.

The prince's laugh rings lightly,
"What road shall we take from home?"
And they answer, "We never shall lose it
If we take the road to Rome."

And with many a jest and banter
The comrades keep their way,
Journeying out of the twilight
Forward into the day,

When they are aware beside them
Goes a pretty minstrel lad,
With a shy and downward aspect,
That is neither sad nor glad.

Over his slender shoulder,
His mandolin was slung,
And around its chords the treasure
Of his golden tresses hung.

Spoke one of the seven companions,
"Little minstrel, whither away?" —
"With seven true-hearted comrades
On their journey, if I may."

Spoke one of the seven companions,
  "If our way be hard and long?"—
"I will lighten it with my music
  And shorten it with my song."

Spoke one of the seven companions,
  "But what are the songs thou know'st?"—
"O, I know many a ditty,
  But this I sing the most:

"How once was an humble maiden
  Beloved of a great lord's son,
That for her sake and his troth's sake
  Was banished and undone.

"And forth of his father's city
  He went at break of day,
And the maiden softly followed
  Behind him on the way

"In the figure of a minstrel,
  And prayed him of his love,
'Let me go with thee and serve thee
  Wherever thou may'st rove.

"'For if thou goest in exile
  I rest banishèd at home,

And where thou wanderest with thee
  My fears in anguish roam,

"'Besetting thy path with perils,
  Making thee hungry and cold,
Filling thy heart with trouble
  And heaviness untold.

"'But let me go beside thee,
  And banishment shall be
Honor, and riches, and country,
  And home to thee and me!'"

Down falls the minstrel-maiden
  Before the Marquis' son,
And the six true-hearted comrades
  Bow round them every one.

Federigo, the son of the Marquis,
  From its scabbard draws his sword:
"Now swear by the honor and fealty
  Ye bear your friend and lord,

"That whenever, and wherever,
  As long as ye have life,
Ye will honor and serve this lady
  As ye would your prince's wife!"

IV.

Over the broad expanses
  Of garlanded Lombardy,
Where the gentle vines are swinging
  In the orchards from tree to tree ;

Through Padua from Verona,
  From the sculptured gothic town,
Carved from ruin upon ruin,
  And ancienter than renown ;

Through Padua from Verona
  To fair Venice, where she stands
With her feet on subject waters,
  Lady of many lands ;

From Venice by sea to Ancona ;
  From Ancona to the west ;
Climbing many a gardened hillside
  And many a castled crest ;

Through valleys dim with the twilight
  Of their gray olive trees ;
Over plains that swim with harvests
  Like golden noonday seas ;

Whence the lofty campanili
  Like the masts of ships arise,

And like a fleet at anchor
  Under them, the village lies;

To Florence beside her Arno,
  In her many-marbled pride,
Crowned with infamy and glory
  By the sons she has denied;

To pitiless Pisa, where never
  Since the anguish of Ugolin
The moon in the Tower of Famine †
  Fate so dread as his hath seen;

Out through the gates of Pisa
  To Livorno on her bay,
To Genoa and to Naples
  The comrades hold their way,

Past the Guelph in his town beleaguered,
  Past the fortressed Ghibelline,
Through lands that reek with slaughter,
  Treason, and shame, and sin;

† "Breve pertugio dentro dalla Muda,
  La qual per me ha il titol della fame
  E in che conviene ancor ch'altri si chiuda,
M'avea mostrato per lo suo forame
  Piu lune gia." DANTE, *L'Inferno.*

By desert, by sea, by city,
  High hill-cope and temple-dome,
Through pestilence, hunger, and horror,
  Upon the road to Rome;

While every land behind them
  Forgets them as they go,
And in Mantua they are remembered
  As is the last year's snow;

But the Marchioness goes to her chamber
  Day after day to weep, —
For the changeless heart of a mother
  The love of a son must keep.

The Marchioness weeps in her chamber
  Over tidings that come to her
Of the exiles she seeks, by letter
  And by lips of messenger,

Broken hints of their sojourn and absence,
  Comfortless, vague, and slight, —
Like feathers wafted backwards
  From passage birds in flight. ‡

‡ "As a feather is wafted downward
  From an eagle in its flight."

The tale of a drunken sailor,
In whose ship they went to sea;
A traveller's evening story
At a village hostelry,

Of certain comrades sent him
By our Lady, of her grace,
To save his life from robbers
In a lonely desert place;

Word from the monks of a convent
Of gentle comrades that lay
One stormy night at their convent,
And passed with the storm at day;

The long parley of a peasant
That sold them wine and food,
The gossip of a shepherd
That guided them through a wood;

A boatman's talk at the ferry
Of a river where they crossed,
And as if they had sunk in the current
All trace of them was lost;

And so is an end of tidings
But never an end of tears,

Of secret and friendless sorrow
  Through blank and silent years.

V.

To the Marchioness in her chamber
  Sends word a messenger,
Newly come from the land of Naples,
  Praying for speech with her.

The messenger stands before her,
  A minstrel slender and wan:
"In a village of my country
  Lies a Mantuan gentleman,

"Sick of a smouldering fever,
  Of sorrow and poverty;
And no one in all that country
  Knows his title or degree.

"But six true Mantuan peasants,
  Or nobles, as some men say,
Watch by the sick man's bedside,
  And toil for him, night and day,

"Hewing, digging, reaping, sowing,
  Bearing burdens, and far and nigh
Begging for him on the highway
  Of the strangers that pass by;

"And they look whenever you meet them
Like broken-hearted men,
And I heard that the sick man would not
If he could, be well again;

"For they say that he for love's sake
Was gladly banishèd,
But she for whom he was banished
Is worse to him, now, than dead, —

"A recreant to his sorrow,
A traitress to his woe."
From her place the Marchioness rises,
The minstrel turns to go.

But fast by the hand she takes him, —
His hand in her clasp is cold, —
"If gold may be thy guerdon
Thou shalt not lack for gold;

"And if the love of a mother
Can bless thee for that thou hast done,
Thou shalt stay and be his brother,
Thou shalt stay and be my son."

"Nay, my lady," answered the minstrel,
And his face is deadly pale,

"Nay, this must not be, sweet lady,
But let my words prevail.

"Let me go now from your presence,
And I will come again,
When you stand with your son beside you,
And be your servant then."

VI.

At the feet of the Marquis Gonzaga
Kneels his lady on the floor;
"Lord, grant me before I ask it
The thing that I implore."

"So it be not of that ingrate." —
"Nay, lord, it is of him."
'Neath the stormy brows of the Marquis
His eyes are tender and dim.

"He lies sick of a fever in Naples,
Near unto death, as they tell,
In his need and pain forsaken
By the wanton he loved so well.

"Now send for him and forgive him,
If ever thou loved'st me,
Now send for him and forgive him
As God shall be good to thee."

"Well so, — if he turn in repentance
And bow himself to my will;
That the high-born lady I chose him
May be my daughter still."

VII.

In Mantua there is feasting
For the Marquis' grace to his son;
In Mantua there is rejoicing
For the prince come back to his own.

The pomp of a wedding procession
Pauses under the pillared porch,
With silken rustle and whisper,
Before the door of the church.

In the midst, Federigo the bridegroom
Stands with his high-born bride;
The six true-hearted comrades
Are three on either side.

The bridegroom is gray as his father,
Where they stand face to face,
And the six true-hearted comrades
Are like old men in their place.

The Marquis takes the comrades
And kisses them one by one:

"That ye were fast and faithful
  And better than I to my son,

"Ye shall be called forever,
  In the sign that ye were so true,
The Faithful of the Gonzaga,
  And your sons after you."

VIII.

To the Marchioness comes a courtier:
  "I am prayed to bring you word
That the minstrel keeps his promise
  Who brought you news of my lord;

"And he waits without the circle
  To kiss your highness' hand;
And he asks no gold for guerdon,
  But before he leaves the land

"He craves of your love once proffered
  That you suffer him for reward,
In this crowning hour of his glory,
  To look on your son, my lord."

Through the silken press of the courtiers
  The minstrel faltered in.
His claspèd hands were bloodless,
  His face was white and thin;

And he bent his knee to the lady,
But of her love and grace
To her heart she raised him and kissed him
Upon his gentle face.

Turned to her son the bridegroom,
Turned to his high-born wife,
"I give you here for your brother
Who gave back my son to life.

"For this youth brought me news from Naples
How thou layest sick and poor,
By true comrades kept, and forsaken
By a false paramour.

"Wherefore I charge you love him
For a brother that is my son."
The comrades turned to the bridegroom
In silence every one.

But the bridegroom looked on the minstrel
With a visage blank and changed,
As his whom the sight of a spectre
From his reason hath estranged;

And the smiling courtiers near them
On a sudden were still as death;

And, subtly-stricken, the people
  Hearkened and held their breath

With an awe uncomprehended
  For an unseen agony : —
Who is this that lies a-dying,
  With her head on the prince's knee ?

A light of anguish and wonder
  Is in the prince's eye,
" O, speak, sweet saint, and forgive me,
  Or I cannot let thee die !

" For now I see thy hardness
  Was softer than mortal ruth,
And thy heavenly guile was whiter,
  My saint, than martyr's truth."

She speaks not and she moves not,
  But a blessèd brightness lies
On her lips in their silent rapture
  And her tender closèd eyes.

Federigo, the son of the Marquis,
  He rises from his knee :
" Aye, you have been good, my father,
  To them that were good to me.

"You have given them honors and titles,
  But here lies one unknown —
Ah, God reward her in heaven
  With the peace he gives his own!"

## THE FIRST CRICKET.

AH me! is it then true that the year has waxed
unto waning,
And that so soon must remain nothing but lapse
and decay, —
Earliest cricket, that out of the midsummer mid-
night complaining,
All the faint summer in me takest with subtle
dismay?

Though thou bringest no dream of frost to the
flowers that slumber,
Though no tree for its leaves, doomed of thy
voice, maketh moan,
Yet with th' unconscious earth's boded evil my
soul thou dost cumber,
And in the year's lost youth makest me still
lose my own.

Answerest thou, that when nights of December are
blackest and bleakest,
And when the fervid grate feigns me a May in
my room,

And by my hearthstone gay, as now sad in my garden, thou creakest, —
  Thou wilt again give me all, — dew and fragrance and bloom ?

Nay, little poet ! full many a cricket I have that is willing,
  If I but take him down out of his place on my shelf,
Me blither lays to sing than the blithest known to thy shrilling,
  Full of the rapture of life, May, morn, hope, and — himself :

Leaving me only the sadder ; for never one of my singers
  Lures back the bee to his feast, calls back the bird to his tree.
Hast thou no art can make me believe, while the summer yet lingers,
  Better than bloom that has been red leaf and sere that must be ?

## THE MULBERRIES.

I.

ON the Rialto Bridge we stand;
The street ebbs under and makes no sound;
But, with bargains shrieked on every hand,
The noisy market rings around.

"*Mulberries, fine mulberries, here!*"
A tuneful voice, — and light, light measure;
Though I hardly should count these mulberries dear,
If I paid three times the price for my pleasure.

Brown hands splashed with mulberry blood,
The basket wreathed with mulberry leaves
Hiding the berries beneath them; — good!
Let us take whatever the young rogue gives.

For you know, old friend, I have n't eaten
A mulberry since the ignorant joy
Of anything sweet in the mouth could sweeten
All this bitter world for a boy.

II.

O, I mind the tree in the meadow stood
By the road near the hill: when I clomb aloof
On its branches, this side of the girdled wood,
I could see the top of our cabin roof.

And, looking westward, could sweep the shores
Of the river where we used to swim
Under the ghostly sycamores,
Haunting the waters smooth and dim;

And eastward athwart the pasture-lot
And over the milk-white buckwheat field
I could see the stately elm, where I shot
The first black squirrel I ever killed.

And southward over the bottom-land
I could see the mellow breadths of farm
From the river-shores to the hills expand,
Clasped in the curving river's arm.

In the fields we set our guileless snares
For rabbits and pigeons and wary quails,
Content with the vaguest feathers and hairs
From doubtful wings and vanished tails.

And in the blue summer afternoon
We used to sit in the mulberry-tree:

The breaths of wind that remembered June
  Shook the leaves and glittering berries free;

And while we watched the wagons go
  Across the river, along the road,
To the mill above, or the mill below,
  With horses that stooped to the heavy load,

We told old stories and made new plans,
  And felt our hearts gladden within us again,
For we did not dream that this life of a man's
  Could ever be what we know as men.

We sat so still that the woodpeckers came
  And pillaged the berries overhead;
From his log the chipmonk, waxen tame,
  Peered, and listened to what we said.

III.

One of us long ago was carried
  To his grave on the hill above the tree;
One is a farmer there, and married;
  One has wandered over the sea.

And, if you ask me, I hardly know
  Whether I'd be the dead or the clown, —
The clod above or the clay below, —
  Or this listless dust by fortune blown

To alien lands. For, however it is,
  So little we keep with us in life :
At best we win only victories,
  Not peace, not peace, O friend, in this strife.

But if I could turn from the long defeat
  Of the little successes once more, and be
A boy, with the whole wide world at my feet,
  Under the shade of the mulberry-tree, —

From the shame of the squandered chances, the sleep
  Of the will that cannot itself awaken,
From the promise the future can never keep,
  From the fitful purposes vague and shaken, —

Then, while the grasshopper sang out shrill
  In the grass beneath the blanching thistle,
And the afternoon air, with a tender thrill,
  Harked to the quail's complaining whistle, —

Ah me ! should I paint the morrows again
  In quite the colors so faint to-day,
And with the imperial mulberry's stain
  Re-purple life's doublet of hodden-gray ?

Know again the losses of disillusion ?
  For the sake of the hope, have the old deceit ? —

In spite of the question's bitter infusion,
  Don't you find these mulberries over-sweet?

All our atoms are changed, they say;
  And the taste is so different since then;
We live, but a world has passed away
  With the years that perished to make us men.

## BEFORE THE GATE.

THEY gave the whole long day to idle laughter,
To fitful song and jest,
To moods of soberness as idle, after,
And silences, as idle too as the rest.

But when at last upon their way returning,
Taciturn, late, and loath,
Through the broad meadow in the sunset burning,
They reached the gate, one fine spell hindered them both.

Her heart was troubled with a subtile anguish
Such as but women know
That wait, and lest love speak or speak not languish,
And what they would, would rather they would not so;

Till he said, — man-like nothing comprehending
Of all the wondrous guile
That women won win themselves with, and bending
Eyes of relentless asking on her the while, —

"Ah, if beyond this gate the path united
  Our steps as far as death,
And I might open it! —" His voice, affrighted
  At its own daring, faltered under his breath.

Then she — whom both his faith and fear enchanted
  Far beyond words to tell,
Feeling her woman's finest wit had wanted
  The art he had that knew to blunder so well —

Shyly drew near, a little step, and mocking,
  "Shall we not be too late
For tea?" she said. "I'm quite worn out with walking:
  Yes, thanks, your arm. And will you — open the gate?"

## CLEMENT.

I.

THAT time of year, you know, when the summer, beginning to sadden,
Full-mooned and silver-misted, glides from the heart of September,
Mourned by disconsolate crickets, and iterant grasshoppers, crying
All the still nights long, from the ripened abundance of gardens;
Then, ere the boughs of the maples are mantled with earliest autumn,
But the wind of autumn breathes from the orchards at nightfall,
Full of winy perfume and mystical yearning and languor;
And in the noonday woods you hear the foraging squirrels,
And the long, crashing fall of the half-eaten nut from the tree-top;
When the robins are mute, and the yellow-birds, haunting the thistles,
Cheep, and twitter, and flit through the dusty lanes and the loppings,

When the pheasant booms from your stealthy
foot in the cornfield,
And the wild-pigeons feed, few and shy, in the
scoke-berry bushes;
When the weary land lies hushed, like a seer in a
vision,
And your life seems but the dream of a dream
which you cannot remember, —
Broken, bewildering, vague, an echo that answers
to nothing!
That time of year, you know. They stood by the
gate in the meadow,
Fronting the sinking sun, and the level stream of
its splendor
Crimsoned the meadow-slope and woodland with
tenderest sunset,
Made her beautiful face like the luminous face of
an angel,
Smote through the painèd gloom of his heart like
a hurt to the sense, there.
Languidly clung about by the half-fallen shawl,
and with folded
Hands, that held a few sad asters: "I sigh for
this idyl
Lived at last to an end; and, looking on to my
prose-life,"
With a smile, she said, and a subtle derision of
manner,

"Better and better I seem, when I recollect all
that has happened
Since I came here in June: the walks we have
taken together
Through these darling meadows, and dear, old,
desolate woodlands;
All our afternoon readings, and all our strolls
through the moonlit
Village, — so sweetly asleep, one scarcely could
credit the scandal,
Heartache, and trouble, and spite, that were hushed
for the night, in its silence.
Yes, I am better. I think I could even be civil to
*him* for his kindness,
Letting me come here without him . . . . . But open
the gate, Cousin Clement;
Seems to me it grows chill, and I think it is
healthier in-doors.
— No, then! you need not speak, for I know well
enough what is coming:
Bitter taunts for the past, and discouraging views
of the future?
Tragedy, Cousin Clement, or comedy, — just as
you like it; —
Only not here alone, but somewhere that people
can see you.
Then I'll take part in the play, and appear the
remorseful young person

Full of divine regrets at not having smothered a genius
Under the feathers and silks of a foolish, extravagant woman.
O you selfish boy! what was it, just now, about anguish?
Bills would be your talk, Cousin Clement, if you were my husband."
  Then, with her summer-night glory of eyes low-bending upon him,
Dark'ning his thoughts as the pondered stars bewilder and darken,
Tenderly, wistfully drooping toward him, she faltered in whisper, —
All her mocking face transfigured, — with mournful effusion:
"Clement, do not think it is you alone that remember, —
Do not think it is you alone that have suffered. Ambition,
Fame, and your art, — you have all these things to console you.
I — what have I? Since my child is dead — a bereavement."
  Sad hung her eyes on his, and he felt all the anger within him
Broken, and melting in tears. But he shrank from her touch while he answered

(Awkwardly, being a man, and awkwardly, being a lover),
"Yes, you know how it is done. You have cleverly fooled me beforetime,
With a dainty scorn, and then an imploring forgiveness!
Yes, you might play it, I think, — that *rôle* of remorseful young person,
That, or the old man's darling, or anything else you attempted.
Even your earnest is so much like acting I fear a betrayal,
Trusting your speech. You say that you have not forgotten. I grant you —
Not, indeed, for your word — that is light — but I wish to believe you.
Well, I say, since you have not forgotten, forget now, forever!
I — I have lived and loved, and you have lived and have married.
Only receive this bud to remember me when we have parted, —
Thorns and splendor, no sweetness, rose of the love that I cherished!"
There he tore from its stalk the imperial flower of the thistle,
Tore, and gave to her, who took it with mocking obeisance,

Twined it in her hair, and said, with her subtle
derision :
"You are a wiser man than I thought you could
ever be, Clement, —
Sensible, almost. So ! I'll try to forget and
remember."
Lightly she took his arm, but on through the lane
to the farm-house,
Mutely together they moved through the lonesome,
odorous twilight.

II.

High on the farm-house hearth, the first autumn
fire was kindled ;
Scintillant hickory bark and dryest limbs of the
beech-tree
Burned, where all summer long the boughs of
asparagus flourished.
Wild were the children with mirth, and grouping
and clinging together,
Danced with the dancing flame, and lithely swayed
with its humor ;
Ran to the window-panes, and peering forth into
the darkness,
Saw there another room, flame-lit, and with frol-
icking children.
(Ah ! by such phantom hearths, I think that we
sit with our first-loves !)

Sometimes they tossed on the floor, and sometimes they hid in the corners,
Shouting and laughing aloud, and never resting a moment,
In the rude delight, the boisterous gladness of childhood, —
Cruel as summer sun and singing-birds to the heartsick.
Clement sat in his chair unmoved in the midst of the hubbub,
Rapt, with unseeing eyes; and unafraid in their gambols,
By his tawny beard the children caught him, and clambered
Over his knees, and waged a mimic warfare across them,
Made him their battle-ground, and won and lost kingdoms upon him.
Airily to and fro, and out of one room to another
Passed his cousin, and busied herself with things of the household,
Nonchalant, debonair, blithe, with bewitching housewifely importance,
Laying the cloth for the supper, and bringing the meal from the kitchen;
Fairer than ever she seemed, and more than ever she mocked him,

Coming behind his chair, and clasping her fingers together
Over his eyes in a girlish caprice, and crying, "Who is it?"
Vexed his despair with a vision of wife and of home and of children,
Calling his sister's children around her, and stilling their clamor,
Making believe they were hers. And Clement sat moody and silent,
Blank to the wistful gaze of his mother bent on his visage
With the tender pain, the pitiful, helpless devotion
Of the mother that looks on the face of her son in his trouble,
Grown beyond her consoling, and knows that she cannot befriend him.
Then his cousin laughed, and in idleness talked with the children;
Sometimes she turned to him, and then when the thistle was falling,
Caught it and twined it again in her hair, and called it her keepsake,
Smiled, and made him ashamed of his petulant gift there, before them.
But, when the night was grown old and the two by the hearthstone together

Sat alone in the flickering red of the flame, and the cricket
Carked to the stillness, and ever, with sullen throbs of the pendule
Sighed the time-worn clock for the death of the days that were perished, —
It was her whim to be sad, and she brought him the book they were reading.
"Read it to-night," she said, "that I may not seem to be going."
Said, and mutely reproached him with all the pain she had wrought him.
From her hand he took the volume and read, and she listened, —
All his voice molten in secret tears, and ebbing and flowing,
Now with a faltering breath, and now with im-impassioned abandon, —
Read from the book of a poet the rhyme of the fatally sundered,
Fatally met too late, and their love was their guilt and their anguish,
But in the night they rose, and fled away into the darkness,
Glad of all dangers and shames, and even of death, for their love's sake.

Then, when his voice brake hollowly, falling and fading to silence,

Thrilled in the silence they sat, and durst not behold one another,
Feeling that wild temptation, that tender, ineffable yearning,
Drawing them heart to heart. One blind, mad moment of passion
With their fate they strove; but out of the pang of the conflict,
Through such costly triumph as wins a waste and a famine,
Victors they came, and Love retrieved the error of loving.
So, foreknowing the years, and sharply discerning the future,
Guessing the riddle of life, and accepting the cruel solution, —
Side by side they sat, as far as the stars are asunder.
Carked the cricket no more, but while the audible silence
Shrilled in their ears, she, suddenly rising and dragging the thistle
Out of her clinging hair, laughed mockingly, casting it from her:
"Perish the thorns and splendor, — the bloom and the sweetness are perished.
Dreary, respectable calm, polite despair, and one's Duty,—

These and the world, for dead Love! — The end
of these modern romances!
Better than yonder rhyme? . . . . Pleasant dreams
and good night, Cousin Clement."

## BY THE SEA.

I WALKED with her I love by the sea,
The deep came up with its chanting waves,
Making a music so great and free
That the will and the faith, which were dead in me,
Awoke and rose from their graves.

Chanting, and with a regal sweep
Of their 'broidered garments up and down
The strand, came the mighty waves of the deep,
Dragging the wave-worn drift from its sleep
Along the sea-sands bare and brown.

" O my soul, make the song of the sea ! " I cried.
" How it comes, with its stately tread,
And its dreadful voice, and the splendid pride
Of its regal garments flowing wide
Over the land !" to my soul I said.

My soul was still ; the deep went down.
" What hast thou, my soul," I cried,
" In thy song ? " " The sea-sands bare and brown,
With broken shells and sea-weed strown,
And stranded drift," my soul replied.

## SAINT CHRISTOPHER.

IN the narrow Venetian street,
On the wall above the garden gate
(Within, the breath of the rose is sweet,
And the nightingale sings there, soon and late),

Stands Saint Christopher, carven in stone,
With the little child in his huge caress,
And the arms of the baby Jesus thrown
About his gigantic tenderness;

And over the wall a wandering growth
Of darkest and greenest ivy clings,
And climbs around them, and holds them both
In its netted clasp of knots and rings,

Clothing the saint from foot to beard
In glittering leaves that whisper and dance
To the child, on his mighty arm upreared,
With a lusty summer exuberance.

To the child on his arm the faithful saint
Looks up with a broad and tranquil joy;

His brows and his heavy beard aslant
  Under the dimpled chin of the boy,

Who plays with the world upon his palm,
  And bends his smiling looks divine
On the face of the giant mild and calm,
  And the glittering frolic of the vine.

He smiles on either with equal grace, —
  On the simple ivy's unconscious life,
And the soul in the giant's lifted face,
  Strong from the peril of the strife :

For both are his own, — the innocence
  That climbs from the heart of earth to heaven,
And the virtue that gently rises thence
  Through trial sent and victory given.

Grow, ivy, up to his countenance,
  But it cannot smile on my life as on thine ;
Look, Saint, with thy trustful, fearless glance,
  Where I dare not lift these eyes of mine.

Venice, 1863.

## ELEGY ON JOHN BUTLER HOWELLS,

Who died, "with the first song of the birds," Wednesday morning, April 27, 1864.

I.

IN the early morning when I wake
At the hour that is sacred for his sake,

And hear the happy birds of spring
In the garden under my window sing,

And through my window the daybreak blows
The sweetness of the lily and rose,

A dormant anguish wakes with day,
And my heart is smitten with strange dismay:

Distance wider than thine, O sea,
Darkens between my brother and me!

II.

A scrap of print, a few brief lines,
The fatal word that swims and shines

On my tears, with a meaning new and dread,
Make faltering reason know him dead,

And I would that my heart might feel it too,
And unto its own regret be true;

For this is the hardest of all to bear,
That his life was so generous and fair,

So full of love, so full of hope,
Broadening out with ample scope,

And so far from death, that his dying seems
The idle agony of dreams

To my heart, that feels him living yet, —
And I forget, and I forget.

III.

He was almost grown a man when he passed
Away, but when I kissed him last

He was still a child, and I had crept
Up to the little room where he slept,

And thought to kiss him good-by in his sleep;
But he was awake to make me weep

With terrible homesickness, before
My wayward feet had passed the door.

Round about me clung his embrace,
And he pressed against my face his face,

As if some prescience whispered him then
That it never, never should be again.

IV.

Out of far-off days of boyhood dim,
When he was a babe and I played with him,

I remember his looks and all his ways;
And how he grew through childhood's grace,

To the hopes, and strifes, and sports, and joys,
And innocent vanity of boys;

I hear his whistle at the door,
His careless step upon the floor,

His song, his jest, his laughter yet, —
And I forget, and I forget.

V.

Somewhere in the graveyard that I know,
Where the strawberries under the chestnuts grow,

They have laid him ; and his sisters set
On his grave the flowers their tears have wet ;

And above his grave, while I write, the song
Of the matin robin leaps sweet and strong

From the leafy dark of the chestnut-tree ;
And many a murmuring honey-bee

On the strawberry blossoms in the grass
Stoops by his grave and will not pass ;

And in the little hollow beneath
The slope of the silent field of death,

The cow-bells tinkle soft and sweet,
And the cattle go by with homeward feet,

And the squirrel barks from the sheltering limb,
At the harmless noises not meant for him ;

And Nature, unto her loving heart
Has taken our darling's mortal part,

Tenderly, that he may be,
Like the song of the robin in the tree,

The blossoms, the grass, the reeds by the shore,
A part of Summer evermore.

VI.

I write, and the words with my tears are wet, —
But I forget, O, I forget!

Teach me, Thou that sendest this pain,
To know and feel my loss and gain!

Let me not falter in belief
On his death, for that is sorest grief:

O, lift me above this wearing strife,
Till I discern his deathless life,

Shining beyond this misty shore,
A part of Heaven evermore.

Venice, Wednesday Morning, at Dawn,
May 16, 1864.

## THANKSGIVING.

I.

LORD, for the erring thought
Not into evil wrought:
Lord, for the wicked will
Betrayed and baffled still:
For the heart from itself kept,
Our thanksgiving accept.

II.

For ignorant hopes that were
Broken to our blind prayer:
For pain, death, sorrow, sent
Unto our chastisement:
For all loss of seeming good,
Quicken our gratitude.

## A SPRINGTIME.

ONE knows the spring is coming :
  There are birds ; the fields are green ;
There is balm in the sunlight and moonlight,
  And dew in the twilights between.

But ever there is a silence,
  A rapture great and dumb,
That day when the doubt is ended,
  And at last the spring is come.

Behold the wonder, O silence !
  Strange as if wrought in a night, —
The waited and lingering glory,
  The world-old, fresh delight !

O blossoms that hang like winter,
  Drifted upon the trees,
O birds that sing in the blossoms,
  O blossom-haunting bees, —

O green, green leaves on the branches,
  O shadowy dark below,

O cool of the aisles of orchards,
  Woods that the wild flowers know, —

O air of gold and perfume,
  Wind, breathing sweet and sun,
O sky of perfect azure —
  Day, Heaven and Earth in one ! —

Let me draw near thy secret,
  And in thy deep heart see
How fared, in doubt and dreaming,
  The spring that is come in me.

For my soul is held in silence,
  A rapture, great and dumb, —
For the mystery that lingered,
  The glory that is come !

1861.

## IN EARLIEST SPRING.

TOSSING his mane of snows in wildest eddies and tangles,
Lion-like, March cometh in, hoarse, with tempestuous breath,
Through all the moaning chimneys, and thwart all the hollows and angles
Round the shuddering house, threating of winter and death.

But in my heart I feel the life of the wood and the meadow
Thrilling the pulses that own kindred with fibres that lift
Bud and blade to the sunward, within the inscrutable shadow,
Deep in the oak's chill core, under the gathering drift.

Nay, to earth's life in mine some prescience, or dream, or desire
(How shall I name it aright?) comes for a moment and goes, —

Rapture of life ineffable, perfect, — as if in the brier,
Leafless there by my door, trembled a sense of the rose.

## THE BOBOLINKS ARE SINGING.

OUT of its frágrant heart of bloom, —
The bobolinks are singing!
Out of its fragrant heart of bloom
The apple-tree whispers to the room,
" Why art thou but a nest of gloom,
While the bobolinks are singing?"

The two wan ghosts of the chamber there, —
The bobolinks are singing!
The two wan ghosts of the chamber there
Cease in the breath of the honeyed air,
Sweep from the room and leave it bare,
While the bobolinks are singing.

Then with a breath so chill and slow, —
The bobolinks are singing!
Then with a breath so chill and slow,
It freezes the blossoms into snow,
The haunted room makes answer low,
While the bobolinks are singing.

"I know that in the meadow-land, —
The bobolinks are singing!
I know that in the meadow-land
The sorrowful, slender elm-trees stand,
And the brook goes by on the other hand,
While the bobolinks are singing.

"But ever I see, in the brawling stream, —
The bobolinks are singing!
But ever I see in the brawling stream
A maiden drowned and floating dim,
Under the water, like a dream,
While the bobolinks are singing.

"Buried, she lies in the meadow-land! —
The bobolinks are singing!
Buried, she lies in the meadow-land,
Under the sorrowful elms where they stand.
Wind, blow over her soft and bland,
While the bobolinks are singing.

"O blow, but stir not the ghastly thing, —
The bobolinks are singing!
O blow, but stir not the ghastly thing
The farmer saw so heavily swing
From the elm, one merry morn of spring,
While the bobolinks were singing.

"O blow, and blow away the bloom, —
  The bobolinks are singing!
O blow, and blow away the bloom
That sickens me in my heart of gloom,
That sweetly sickens the haunted room,
  While the bobolinks are singing!"

## PRELUDE.

(TO AN EARLY BOOK OF VERSE.)

IN March the earliest bluebird came
 And caroled from the orchard-tree
 His little tremulous songs to me,
And called upon the summer's name.

And made old summers in my heart
 All sweet with flower and sun again;
 So that I said, "O, not in vain
Shall be thy lay of little art,

" Though never summer sun may glow,
 Nor summer flower for thee may bloom;
 Though winter turn in sudden gloom,
And drowse the stirring spring with snow";

And learned to trust, if I should call
 Upon the sacred name of Song,
 Though chill through March I languish long,
And never feel the May at all,

Yet may I touch, in some who hear,
  The hearts, wherein old songs asleep
  Wait but the feeblest touch to leap
In music sweet as summer air!

I sing in March brief bluebird lays,
  And hope a May, and do not know:
  May be, the heaven is full of snow, —
May be, there open summer days.

## THE MOVERS.

SKETCH.

PARTING was over at last, and all the good-bys had been spoken.
Up the long hillside road the white-tented wagon moved slowly,
Bearing the mother and children, while onward before them the father
Trudged with his gun on his arm, and the faithful house-dog beside him,
Grave and sedate, as if knowing the sorrowful thoughts of his master.

April was in her prime, and the day in its dewy awaking:
Like a great flower, afar on the crest of the eastern woodland,
Goldenly bloomed the sun, and over the beautiful valley,
Dim with its dew and shadow, and bright with its dream of a river,

Looked to the western hills, and shone on the humble procession,
Paining with splendor the children's eyes, and the heart of the mother.

Beauty, and fragrance, and song filled the air like a palpable presence.
Sweet was the smell of the dewy leaves and the flowers in the wild-wood,
Fair the long reaches of sun and shade in the aisles of the forest.
Glad of the spring, and of love, and of morning, the wild birds were singing :
Jays to each other called harshly, then mellowly fluted together ;
Sang the oriole songs as golden and gay as his plumage ;
Pensively piped the querulous quails their greetings unfrequent,
While, on the meadow elm, the meadow lark gushed forth in music,
Rapt, exultant, and shaken with the great joy of his singing ;
Over the river, loud-chattering, aloft in the air, the kingfisher
Hung, ere he dropped like a bolt, in the water beneath him ;

Gossiping, out of the bank flew myriad twittering swallows;
And in the boughs of the sycamores quarrelled and clamored the blackbirds.

Never for these things a moment halted the Movers, but onward,
Up the long hillside road the white-tented wagon moved slowly.
Till, on the summit, that overlooked all the beautiful valley,
Trembling and spent, the horses came to a standstill unbidden;
Then from the wagon the mother in silence got down with her children,
Came, and stood by the father, and rested her hand on his shoulder.

Long together they gazed on the beautiful valley before them;
Looked on the well-known fields that stretched away to the woodlands,
Where, in the dark lines of green, showed the milk-white crest of the dogwood,
Snow of wild-plums in bloom, and crimson tints of the red-bud;

Looked on the pasture-fields where the cattle were lazily grazing, —
Soft, and sweet, and thin came the faint, far notes of the cow-bells, —
Looked on the oft-trodden lanes, with their elder and blackberry borders,
Looked on the orchard, a bloomy sea, with its billows of blossoms.
Fair was the scene, yet suddenly strange and all unfamiliar,
As are the faces of friends, when the word of farewell has been spoken.
Long together they gazed; then at last on the little log-cabin —
Home for so many years, now home no longer forever —
Rested their tearless eyes in the silent rapture of anguish.
Up on the morning air no column of smoke from the chimney
Wavering, silver and azure, rose, fading and brightening ever;
Shut was the door where yesterday morning the children were playing;
Lit with a gleam of the sun the window stared up at them blindly.
Cold was the hearthstone now, and the place was forsaken and empty.

Empty? Ah no! but haunted by thronging and tenderest fancies,
Sad recollections of all that had been, of sorrow or gladness.

Still they sat there in the glow of the wide red fire in the winter,
Still they sat there by the door in the cool of the still summer evening,
Still the mother seemed to be singing her babe there to slumber,
Still the father beheld her weep o'er the child that was dying,
Still the place was haunted by all the Past's sorrow and gladness!

Neither of them might speak for the thoughts that came crowding their hearts so,
Till, in their ignorant trouble aloud the children lamented;
Then was the spell of silence dissolved, and the father and mother
Burst into tears and embraced, and turned their dim eyes to the Westward.

Ohio, 1859.

## THROUGH THE MEADOW.

THE summer sun was soft and bland,
As they went through the meadow land.

The little wind that hardly shook
The silver of the sleeping brook
Blew the gold hair about her eyes, —
A mystery of mysteries!
So he must often pause, and stoop,
And all the wanton ringlets loop
Behind her dainty ear — emprise
Of slow event and many sighs.

Across the stream was scarce a step, —
And yet she feared to try the leap;
And he, to still her sweet alarm,
Must lift her over on his arm.

She could not keep the narrow way,
For still the little feet would stray,
And ever must he bend t' undo
The tangled grasses from her shoe, —

From dainty rosebud lips in pout,
Must kiss the perfect flowér out!

Ah! little coquette! Fair deceit!
Some things are bitter that were sweet.

## GONE.

IS it the shrewd October wind
  Brings the tears into her eyes?
Does it blow so strong that she must fetch
  Her breath in sudden sighs?

The sound of his horse's feet grows faint,
  The Rider has passed from sight;
The day dies out of the crimson west,
  And coldly falls the night.

She presses her tremulous fingers tight
  Against her closéd eyes,
And on the lonesome threshold there,
  She cowers down and cries.

## THE SARCASTIC FAIR.

HER mouth is a honey-blossom,
  No doubt, as the poet sings;
But within her lips, the petals,
  Lurks a cruel bee, that stings.

## RAPTURE.

IN my rhyme I fable anguish,
   Feigning that my love is dead,
Playing at a game of sadness,
   Singing hope forever fled, —

Trailing the slow robes of mourning,
   Grieving with the player's art,
With the languid palms of sorrow
   Folded on a dancing heart.

I must mix my love with death-dust,
   Lest the draught should make me mad;
I must make believe at sorrow,
   Lest I perish, over-glad.

## DEAD.

I.

SOMETHING lies in the room
  Over against my own;
The windows are lit with a ghastly bloom
  Of candles, burning alone, —
Untrimmed, and all aflare
In the ghastly silence there !

II.

People go by the door,
  Tiptoe, holding their breath,
And hush the talk that they held before,
  Lest they should waken Death,
That is awake all night
There in the candlelight !

III.

The cat upon the stairs
  Watches with flamy eye
For the sleepy one who shall unawares
  Let her go stealing by.

She softly, softly purrs,
And claws at the banisters.

IV.

The bird from out its dream
  Breaks with a sudden song,
That stabs the sense like a sudden scream;
  The hound the whole night long
Howls to the moonless sky,
So far, and starry, and high.

## THE DOUBT.

SHE sits beside the low window,
  In the pleasant evening-time,
With her face turned to the sunset,
  Reading a book of rhyme.

And the wine-light of the sunset,
  Stolen into the dainty nook,
Where she sits in her sacred beauty,
  Lies crimson on the book.

O beautiful eyes so tender,
  Brown eyes so tender and dear,
Did you leave your reading a moment
  Just now, as I passed near?

Maybe, 't is the sunset flushes
  Her features, so lily-pale;
Maybe, 't is the lover's passion,
  She reads of in the tale.

O darling, and darling, and darling,
  If I dared to trust my thought;

If I dared to believe what I must not,
  Believe what no one ought, —

We would read together the poem
  Of the Love that never died,
The passionate, world-old story
  Come true, and glorified.

## THE THORN.

"EVERY Rose, you sang, has its Thorn,
  But this has none, I know."
She clasped my rival's Rose
  Over her breast of snow.

I bowed to hide my pain,
  With a man's unskilful art;
I moved my lips, and could not say
  The Thorn was in my heart!

## THE MYSTERIES.

ONCE on my mother's breast, a child, I crept,
  Holding my breath;
There, safe and sad, lay shuddering, and wept
  At the dark mystery of Death.

Weary and weak, and worn with all unrest,
  Spent with the strife, —
O mother, let me weep upon thy breast
  At the sad mystery of Life!

## THE BATTLE IN THE CLOUDS.

"The day had been one of dense mists and rains, and much of General Hooker's battle was fought above the clouds, on the top of Lookout Mountain." — GENERAL MEIG'S *Report of the Battle before Chattanooga.*

WHERE the dews and the rains of heaven
have their fountain,
Like its thunder and its lightning our brave
burst on the foe,
Up above the clouds on Freedom's Lookout Moun-
tain
Raining life-blood like water on the valleys down
below.
O, green be the laurels that grow,
O sweet be the wild-buds that blow,
In the dells of the mountain where the brave
are lying low.

Light of our hope and crown of our story,
Bright as sunlight, pure as starlight shall their
deeds of daring glow,
While the day and the night out of heaven shed
their glory,

On Freedom's Lookout Mountain whence they
routed Freedom's foe.
O, soft be the gales when they go
Through the pines on the summit where
they blow,
Chanting solemn music for the souls that passed
below.

## FOR ONE OF THE KILLED.

THERE on the field of battle
Lies the young warrior dead :
Who shall speak in the soldier's honor ?
How shall his praise be said ?

Cannon, there in the battle,
Thundered the soldier's praise,
Hark ! how the volumed volleys echo
Down through the far-off days !

Tears for the grief of a father,
For a mother's anguish, tears ;
But for him that died in his country's battle,
Glory and endless years.

## THE TWO WIVES.

(TO COLONEL J. G. M., IN MEMORY OF THE EVENT BEFORE ATLANTA.)

I.

THE colonel rode by his picket-line
  In the pleasant morning sun,
That glanced from him far off to shine
  On the crouching rebel picket's gun.

II.

From his command the captain strode
  Out with a grave salute,
And talked with the colonel as he rode; —
  The picket levelled his piece to shoot.

III.

The colonel rode and the captain walked, —
  The arm of the picket tired;
Their faces almost touched as they talked,
  And, swerved from his aim, the picket fired.

IV.

The captain fell at the horse's feet,
  Wounded and hurt to death,

Calling upon a name that was sweet
As God is good, with his dying breath.

V.

And the colonel that leaped from his horse and knelt
To close the eyes so dim,
A high remorse for God's mercy felt,
Knowing the shot was meant for him.

VI.

And he whispered, prayer-like, under his breath,
The name of his own young wife :
For Love, that had made his friend's peace with Death,
Alone could make his with life.

## BEREAVED.

THE passionate humming-birds cling
  To the honeysuckles' hearts;
In and out at the open window
  The twittering house-wren darts,
        And the sun is bright.

June is young, and warm, and sweet;
  The morning is gay and new;
Glimmers yet the grass of the door-yard,
  Pearl-gray with fragrant dew,
        And the sun is bright.

From the mill, upon the stream,
  A busy murmur swells;
On to the pasture go the cattle,
  Lowing, with tinkling bells,
        And the sun is bright.

She gathers his playthings up,
  And dreamily puts them by;
Children are playing in the meadow,
  She hears their joyous cry,
        And the sun is bright.

She sits and clasps her brow,
  And looks with swollen eyes
On the landscape that reels and dances, —
  To herself she softly cries,
      And the sun is bright.

## THE SNOW-BIRDS.

THE lonesome graveyard lieth,
  A deep with silent waves
Of night-long snow, all white, and billowed
  Over the hidden graves.

The snow-birds come in the morning,
  Flocking and fluttering low,
And light on the graveyard brambles,
  And twitter there in the snow.

The Singer, old and weary,
  Looks out from his narrow room :
" Ah, me ! but my thoughts are snow-birds,
  Haunting a graveyard gloom,

" Where all the Past is buried
  And dead, these many years,
Under the drifted whiteness
  Of frozen falls of tears.

" Poor birds ! that know not summer,
  Nor sun, nor flowèrs fair, —
Only the graveyard brambles,
  And graves, and winter air ! "

## VAGARY.

UP and down the dusty street,
I hurry with my burning feet;
Against my face the wind-waves beat,
Fierce from the city-sea of heat.
Deep in my heart the vision is,
Of meadow grass and meadow trees
Blown silver in the summer breeze,
And ripe, red, hillside strawberries.

My sense the city tumult fills, —
The tumult that about me reels
Of strokes and cries, and feet and wheels.
Deep in my dream I list, and, hark!
From out the maple's leafy dark,
The fluting of the meadow lark!

About the throngèd street I go:
There is no face here that I know;
Of all that pass me to and fro
There is no face here that I know.
Deep in my soul's most sacred place,
With a sweet pain I look and trace
The features of a tender face,
All lit with love and girlish grace.

Some spell is on me, for I seem
A memory of the past, a dream
Of happiness remembered dim,
    Unto myself that walk the street
    Scathed with the city's noontide heat,
    With puzzled brain and burning feet.

## FEUERBILDER.

THE children sit by the fireside
  With their little faces in bloom;
And behind, the lily-pale mother,
  Looking out of the gloom,

Flushes as if a rosebud
  Were bursting in her heart;
But the father sits there silent,
  From the firelight apart.

"Now, what dost thou see in the embers?
  Tell it to me, my child,"
Whispers the lily-pale mother
  To her daughter sweet and mild.

"O, I see a sky and a moon
  In the coals and ashes there,
And under, two are walking
  In a garden of flowers so fair.

"A lady gay, and her lover,
  Talking with low-voiced words,

Not to waken the dreaming flowers
And the sleepy little birds."

Back in the gloom the mother
Shrinks with a sudden sigh.
"Now, what dost thou see in the embers?"
Cries the father to the boy.

"O, I see a wedding-procession
Go in at the church's door, —
Ladies in silks and knights in steel, —
A hundred of them, and more.

"The bride's face is as white as a lily,
And the groom's head is white as snow;
And without, with plumes and tapers,
A funeral paces slow."

Loudly then laughed the father,
And shouted again for cheer,
And called to the drowsy housemaid
To fetch him a pipe and beer.

# AVERY.

[NIAGARA, 1853.]

I.

ALL night long they heard in the houses beside the shore,
Heard, or seemed to hear, through the multitudinous roar,
Out of the hell of the rapids as 't were a lost soul's cries, —
Heard and could not believe; and the morning mocked their eyes,
Showing, where wildest and fiercest the waters leaped up and ran
Raving round him and past, the visage of a man
Clinging, or seeming to cling, to the trunk of a tree that, caught
Fast in the rocks below, scarce out of the surges raught.
Was it a life, could it be, to yon slender hope that clung?
Shrill, above all the tumult the answering terror rung.

II.

Under the weltering rapids a boat from the bridge
is drowned,
Over the rocks the lines of another are tangled
and wound;
And the long, fateful hours of the morning have
wasted soon,
As it had been in some blessed trance, and now it
is noon.
Hurry, now with the raft! But O, build it strong
and stanch,
And to the lines and treacherous rocks look well as
you launch!
Over the foamy tops of the waves, and their foam-
sprent sides,
Over the hidden reefs, and through the embattled
tides,
Onward rushes the raft, with many a lurch and
leap, —
Lord! if it strike him loose from the hold he
scarce can keep!

No! through all peril unharmed, it reaches him
harmless at last,
And to its proven strength he lashes his weakness
fast.

Now, for the shore! But steady, steady, my men,
  and slow;
Taut, now, the quivering lines; now slack; and
  so, let her go!
Thronging the shores around stand the pitying
  multitude;
Wan as his own are their looks, and a nightmare
  seems to brood
Heavy upon them, and heavy the silence hangs
  on all,
Save for the rapids' plunge, and the thunder of
  the fall.
But on a sudden thrills from the people still and
  pale,
Chorussing his unheard despair, a desperate wail:
Caught on a lurking point of rock it sways and
  swings,
Sport of the pitiless waters, the raft to which he
  clings.

III.

All the long afternoon it idly swings and sways;
And on the shore the crowd lifts up its hands and
  prays:
Lifts to heaven and wrings the hands so helpless
  to save,

Prays for the mercy of God on him whom the rock and the wave
Battle for, fettered betwixt them, and who, amidst their strife,
Struggles to help his helpers, and fights so hard for his life, —
Tugging at rope and at reef, while men weep and women swoon.
Priceless second by second, so wastes the afternoon,
And it is sunset now ; and another boat and the last
Down to him from the bridge through the rapids has safely passed.

IV.

Wild through the crowd comes flying a man that nothing can stay,
Maddening against the gate that is locked athwart his way.
"No ! we keep the bridge for them that can help him. You,
Tell us, who are you ?" "His brother !" "God help you both ! Pass through."
Wild, with wide arms of imploring he calls aloud to him,

Unto the face of his brother, scarce seen in the distance dim ;
But in the roar of the rapids his fluttering words are lost
As in a wind of autumn the leaves of autumn are tossed.
And from the bridge he sees his brother sever the rope
Holding him to the raft, and rise secure in his hope ;
Sees all as in a dream the terrible pageantry, —
Populous shores, the woods, the sky, the birds flying free ;
Sees, then, the form, — that, spent with effort and fasting and fear,
Flings itself feebly and fails of the boat that is lying so near, —
Caught in the long-baffled clutch of the rapids, and rolled and hurled
Headlong on to the cataract's brink, and out of the world.

## BOPEEP: A PASTORAL.

"O, to what uses shall we put
The wildweed flower that simply blows?
And is there any moral shut
Within the bosom of the rose?"

TENNYSON.

I.

SHE lies upon the soft, enamoured grass,
I' the wooing shelter of an apple-tree,
And at her feet the trancéd brook is glass,
And in the blossoms over her the bee
Hangs charméd of his sordid industry;
For love of her the light wind will not pass.

II.

Her golden hair, blown over her red lips,
That seem two rose-leaves softly breathed apart,
Athwart her rounded throat like sunshine slips;
Her small hand, resting on her beating heart,
The crook that tells her peaceful shepherd-art
Scarce keeps with light and tremulous finger-tips.

III.

She is as fair as any shepherdess
That ever was in mask or Christmas scene:

Bright silver spangles hath she on her dress,
  And of her red-heeled shoes appears the sheen;
  And she hath ribbons of such blue or green
As best suits pastoral people's comeliness.

IV.

She sleeps, and it is in the month of May,
  And the whole land is full of the delight
Of music and sweet scents; and all the day
  The sun is gold; the moon is pearl all night,
  And like a paradise the world is bright,
And like a young girl's hopes the world is gay.

V.

So waned the hours; and while her beauteous sleep
  Was blest with many a happy dream of Love,
Untended still, her silly, vagrant sheep
  Afar from that young shepherdess did rove,
  Along the vales and through the gossip grove,
O'er daisied meads and up the thymy steep.

VI.

Then (for it happens oft when harm is nigh,
  Our dreams grow haggard till at last we wake)
She thought that from the little runnel by
  There crept upon a sudden forth a snake,
  And stung her hand, and fled into the brake;
Whereat she sprang up with a bitter cry,

VII.

And wildly over all that place did look,
  And could not spy her ingrate, wanton flock, —
Not there among tall grasses by the brook,
  Not there behind the mossy-bearděd rock;
  And pitiless Echo answered with a mock
When she did sorrow that she was forsook.

VIII.

Alas! the scattered sheep might not be found,
  And long and loud that gentle maid did weep,
Till in her blurréd sight the hills went round,
  And, circling far, field, wood, and stream did
    sweep;
  And on the ground the miserable Bopeep
Fell and forgot her troubles in a swound.

IX.

When she awoke, the sun long time had set,
  And all the land was sleeping in the moon,
And all the flowers with dim, sad dews were wet,
  As they had wept to see her in that swoon.
  It was about the night's low-breathing noon;
Only the larger stars were waking yet.

X.

Bopeep, the fair and hapless shepherdess,
  Rose from her swooning in a sore dismay,

And tried to smooth her damp and rumpled dress,
 That showed in truth a grievous disarray;
 Then where the brook the wan moon's mirror lay,
She laved her eyes, and curled each golden tress.

XI.

And looking to her ribbons, if they were
 As ribbons of a shepherdess should be,
She took the hat that she was wont to wear
 (Bedecked it was with ribbons flying free
 As ever man in opera might see),
And set it on her curls of yellow hair.

XII.

"And I will go and seek my sheep," she said,
 "Through every distant land until I die;
But when they bring me hither, cold and dead,
 Let me beneath these apple-blossoms lie,
 With this dear, faithful, lovely runnel nigh,
Here, where my cru — cru — cruel sheep have fed."

XIII.

Thus sorrow and despair make bold Bopeep,
 And forth she springs, and hurries on her way:
Across the lurking rivulet she can leap,
 No sombre forest shall her quest delay,
 No crooked vale her eager steps bewray:
What dreadeth she that seeketh her lost sheep?

XIV.

By many a pond, where timorous water-birds,
  With clattering cries and throbbing wings, arose,
By many a pasture, where the soft-eyed herds
  Looked shadow-huge in their unmoved repose,
  Long through the lonesome night that sad one goes
And fills the solitude with wailing words;

XV.

So that the little field-mouse dreams of harm,
  Snuggled away from harm beneath the weeds;
The violet, sleeping on the clover's arm,
  Wakes, and is cold with thoughts of dreadful deeds;
  The pensive people of the water-reeds
Hark with a mute and dolorous alarm.

XVI.

And the fond hearts of all the turtle-doves
  Are broken in compassion of her woe,
And every tender little bird that loves
  Feels in his breast a sympathetic throe;
  And flowers are sad wherever she may go,
And hoarse with sighs the waterfalls and groves.

XVII.

The pale moon droppeth low; star after star
Grows faint and slumbers in the gray of dawn;
And still she lingers not, but hurries far,
Till in a dreary wilderness withdrawn
Through tangled woods she lorn and lost moves on,
Where griffins dire and dreadful dragons are.

XVIII.

Her ribbons all are dripping with the dew,
Her red-heeled shoes are torn, and stained with mire,
Her tender arms the angry sharpness rue
Of many a scraggy thorn and envious brier;
And poor Bopeep, with no sweet pity nigh her,
Wrings her small hands, and knows not what to do.

XIX.

And on that crude and rugged ground she sinks,
And soon her seeking had been ended there,
But through the trees a fearful glimmer shrinks,
And of a hermit's dwelling she is 'ware:
At the dull pane a dull-eyed taper blinks,
Drowsed with long vigils and the morning air.

XX.

Thither she trembling moves, and at the door
  Falls down, and cannot either speak or stir :
The hermit comes, — with no white beard before,
  Nor coat of skins, nor cap of shaggy fur :
  It was a comely youth that lifted her,
And to his hearth, and to his breakfast, bore.

XXI.

Arrayed he was in princeliest attire,
  And of as goodly presence sooth was he
As any little maiden might admire,
  Or any king-beholding cat might see
  "My poor Bopeep," he sigheth piteously,
"Rest here, and warm you at a hermit's fire."

XXII.

She looked so beautiful, there, mute and white,
  He kissed her on the lips and on the eyes
(The most a prince could do in such a plight) ;
  But chiefly gazed on her in still surprise,
  And when he saw her lily eyelids rise,
For him the whole world had no fairer sight.

XXIII.

"Rude is my fare : a bit of venison steak,
  A dish of honey and a glass of wine,

With clean white bread, is the poor feast I make.
  Be served, I pray : I think this flask is fine,"
  He said. " Hard is this hermit life of mine :
This day I will its weariness forsake."

XXIV.

And then he told her how it chanced that he,
  King Cole's son, in that forest held his court,
And the sole reason that there seemed to be
  Was, he was being hermit there for sport ;
  But he confessed the life was not his forte,
And therewith both laughed out right jollily.

XXV.

And sly Bopeep forgot her sheep again
  In gay discourse with that engaging youth :
Love hath such sovran remedies for pain !
  But then he was a handsome prince, in truth,
  And both were young, and both were silly, sooth,
And everything to Love but love seems vain.

XXVI.

They took them down the silver-claspéd book
  That this young anchorite's predecessor kept, —
A holy seer, — and through it they did look ;

Sometimes their idle eyes together crept,
Sometimes their lips; but still the leaves they swept,
Until they found a shepherd's pictured crook.

XXVII.

And underneath was writ it should befall
On such a day, in such a month and year,
A maiden fair, a young prince brave and tall,
By such a chance should come together here.
They were the people, that was very clear:
"O love," the prince said, "let us read it all!"

XXVIII.

And thus the hermit's prophecy ran on:
Though she her lost sheep wist not where to find,
Yet should she bid her weary care begone,
And banish every doubt from her sweet mind:
They, with their little snow-white tails behind,
Homeward would go, if they were left alone.

XXIX.

They closed the book, and in her happy eyes
The prince read truth and love forevermore, —
Better than any hermit's prophecies!
They passed together from the cavern's door;
Embraced, they turned to look at it once more,
And over it beheld the glad sun rise,

XXX.

That streamed before them aisles of dusk and gold
 Under the song-swept arches of the wood,
And forth they went, tranced in each other's hold,
 Down through that rare and luminous solitude,
 Their happy hearts enchanted in the mood
Of morning, and of May, and romance old.

XXXI.

Sometimes the saucy leaves would kiss her cheeks,
 And he must kiss their wanton kiss away;
To die beneath her feet the wood-flower seeks,
 The quivering aspen feels a fine dismay,
 And many a scented blossom on the spray
In odorous sighs its passionate longing speaks.

XXXII.

And forth they went down to that stately stream,
 Bowed over by the ghostly sycamores
(Awearily, as if some heavy dream
 Held them in languor), but whose opulent shores
 With pearlèd shells and dusts of precious ores
Were tremulous brilliance in the morning beam;

XXXIII.

Where waited them, beside the lustrous sand,
 A silk-winged shallop, sleeping on the flood;

And smoothly wafted from the hither strand,
  Across the calm, broad stream they lightly rode,
  Under them still the silver fishes stood;
The eager lilies, on the other land,

XXXIV.

Beckonéd them; but where the castle shone
  With diamonded turrets and a wall
Of gold-embedded pearl and costly stone,
  Their vision to its peerless splendor thrall
  The maiden fair, the young prince brave and tall,
Thither with light, unlingering feet pressed on.

XXXV.

A gallant train to meet this loving pair,
  In silk and steel, moves from the castle door,
And up the broad and ringing castle stair
  They go with gleeful minstrelsy before,
  And "Hail our prince and princess evermore!"
From all the happy throng is greeting there.

XXXVI.

And in the hall the prince's sire, King Cole,
  Sitting with crown and royal ermine on,
His fiddlers three behind with pipe and bowl,
  Rises and moves to lift his kneeling son,
  Greeting his bride with kisses many a one,
And tears and laughter from his jolly soul;

XXXVII.

Then both his children to a window leads
  That over daisied pasture-land looks out,
And shows Bopeep where her lost flock wide feeds,
  And every frolic lambkin leaps about.
  She hears Boy-Blue, that lazy shepherd, shout,
Slow pausing from his pipe of mellow reeds;

XXXVIII.

And, turning, peers into her prince's eyes;
  Then, caught and clasped against her prince's heart,
Upon her breath her answer wordless dies,
  And leaves her gratitude to sweeter art, —
  To lips from which the bloom shall never part,
To looks wherein the summer never dies!

## WHILE SHE SANG.

I.

SHE sang, and I heard the singing,
  Far out of the wretched past,
Of meadow-larks in the meadow,
  In a breathing of the blast.

Cold through the clouds of sunset
  The thin red sunlight shone,
Staining the gloom of the woodland
  Where I walked and dreamed alone;

And glinting with chilly splendor
  The meadow under the hill,
Where the lingering larks were lurking
  In the sere grass hid and still.

Out they burst with their singing,
  Their singing so loud and gay;
They made in the heart of October
  A sudden ghastly May,

That faded and ceased with their singing.
  The thin red sunlight paled,

And through the boughs above me
  The wind of evening wailed; —

Wailed, and the light of evening
  Out of the heaven died;
And from the marsh by the river
  The lonesome killdee cried.

II.

The song is done, but a phantom
  Of music haunts the chords,
That thrill with its subtile presence,
  And grieve for the dying words.

And in the years that are perished,
  Far back in the wretched past,
I see on the May-green meadows
  The white snow falling fast; —

Falling, and falling, and falling,
  As still and cold as death,
On the bloom of the odorous orchard,
  On the small, meek flowers beneath;

On the roofs of the village-houses,
  On the long, silent street,
Where its plumes are soiled and broken
  Under the passing feet;

On the green crest of the woodland,
  On the cornfields far apart;
On the cowering birds in the gable,
  And on my desolate heart.

## NAMING THE BIRD.

(FRAGMENT.)

I.

THEY bring the new canary forth,
  They hang his cage against the pane
  Sunlit, and looking where the vane
Veers southward from the yielding north.

Against the pane the creepers press
  Their dank, dead leaves; the light wind goes
  Through all the dwarfish pines, and blows
The tendrils from their weak caress.

The light wind whispers at the pane,
  Of summer, and the bird within,
  That hears the careless breeze begin,
Bursts loud above the vaguer strain

With such a song of happy June,
  That sunward sward and lingering snow
  Green billowy grasses overflow,
And from the heaven falls a noon

Of languor and of still delight;
  The locust-trees are white with blooms

And through their drifted blossom booms
The summer bee in golden flight.

"O now he sings us something good,
The bird that yet has won no name,"
They say, "as if the singer's fame
Were last and least of all he would!

"But let us name him now," and bowed,
In thought, their dark and golden hair,
Their faces differently fair
Together, while the bird sang loud.

He sang of nothing, but they made
His song a meaning as before,
And life and death the meaning bore,
And through the soulless carol played

All sadness of the soul of youth,
All sweetness of their girlhood's prime,
All joy and grief of other time,
All dreamy pain and tender ruth.

It made them think of long ago, —
In youth the dead months measure years, —
It filled their soft girl-hearts with tears,
Their eyes with pensive overflow.

They rose, and with such gracious ways
  As women use, whose souls are wed,
  They kissed each other, and they said,
"O, let us call him Other Days!

"And Daysie, for the flower's sake,
  Or Daysie, for some stupid friend
  Would find it hard to comprehend
The larger meaning that we take

From Other Days." "But now," she cried, —
  The dark-eyed to the eyes of blue, —
  "Sing that old song was made for you
In other days, — in merrier tide."

And swept to the piano-seat,
  And swiftly struck the startled keys;
  The other mused old melodies,
Then sang with mockery strange and sweet:

II.

Other days shall come and go,
  Other days are gone,
Let the restless river flow,
  For it bears us on
    Together, —

Slow to find the unknown sea,
Wandering thorough wold and steep and lea,
  But it bears us thither.
    Ah, whither?

Other days shall come and go,
  Other days are gone.
Love, I find it hard to know
  What is lost and won
    Forever.
Out of rapture stēaleth sorrow,
Yesterday will sadly haunt to-morrow,
  Pain from love shall sever,
    Ah, never!

Other days, and they were young,
  They whose blood is cold;
They forgot the songs they sung
  In the days of old.
    Aweary,
Love nor anguish they regret.
Let us die, O love, ere we forget
  Sunny days with dreary,
    We weary!

III.

The song was made in other time
  In other time, when he who mocked
  His daring hope with sadness walked
All day in dreams of love and rhyme ;

And he who let the days depart
  In idle reveries that flowed
  From dreams to bitter waking, snowed
His own tears back upon his heart :

IV.

Good by ! We part. I do not know
  Whether we part for good or ill ;
Life's great results are something slow,
  But friendly doubt attends us still.

I notice fickleness of weather
  In that strange climate of the heart :
People forget love when together, —
  I think we won't do worse apart.

V.

With absent hands she touched the keys
  That trembled yet from other hands,

With absent thoughts of far-off lands
Beyond the unrest of death-wide seas.

She played old tunes, she vaguely mused,
She poured her soul into the strain
That passed from rapture into pain,
With love and mocking interfused,

And rose in swelling harmony,
And from its full and joyous tide
Ebbed into languid doubt, and died
Away from voice and chord and key.

Full loud the bird's blithe carol rang
In bursts of wild and fluttering song,
And with her music borne along,
Above his art he strove and sang.

But with the silence through the room
A shadow stole, and from the east
The thin, faint smile of sunshine ceased,
And all the day was dipped in gloom.

A gust of cold and sudden rain
Swept down on sward and lingering snow,
And in the weird wind to and fro
Struck blinding tears against the pane.

VI.

With plaintive chirp and quaint bird-ways
  Of prim-set wings and sidelong head,
  The bird looked wonder; but they said,
"O, well we named him Other Days!

"For Other Days that were so glad,
  For thoughts and dreams and songs of yore;
  For Other Days that come no more,
Or only come to make us sad."

## A POET.

FROM wells where Truth in secret lay
He saw the midnight stars by day.

"O marvellous gift!" the many cried,
"O cruel gift!" his voice replied.

The stars were far, and cold, and high,
That glimmered in the noonday sky;

He yearned toward the sun in vain,
That warmed the lives of other men.

## CONVENTION.

HE falters on the threshold,
She lingers on the stair :
Can it be that was his footstep ?
Can it be that she is there ?

Without is tender yearning,
And tender love is within ;
They can hear each other's heart-beats,
But a wooden door is between.

## THE POET'S FRIENDS.

THE robin sings in the elm ;
The cattle stand beneath,
Sedate and grave, with great brown eyes
And fragrant meadow-breath.

They listen to the flattered bird,
The wise-looking, stupid things ;
And they never understand a word
Of all the robin sings.

THE END.

Cambridge : Printed by Welch, Bigelow, & Co.

www.ingramcontent.com/pod-product-compliance
Lightning Source LLC
LaVergne TN
LVHW011238110826
845150LV00006B/1671

* 9 7 8 1 4 2 5 5 1 3 6 7 2 *